Alternative Life-Styles Confront the Church

Alternative Life-Styles Confront the Church

DEANE WILLIAM FERM

The Seabury Press / New York

To
Bill, Nin, and Ned
Lin
Bob
Laurie
     and their life-styles.
     GOOD BOS!

1983
The Seabury Press
815 Second Avenue
New York, N.Y. 10017

Printed in the United States of America

Library of Congress Cataloging in Publication Data

Ferm, Deane William, 1927–
    Alternative life-styles confront the church.

    1. Church and social problems—United States.
2. United States—Moral conditions.   3. Christian
life—1960-   . I. Title.
HN39.U6F47 1983   261.8'34   82-17038
ISBN 0-8164-2394-6 (pbk.)

•Contents

Preface

Everyone knows that we are in the midst of a profound moral and social revolution. Old norms for behavior are shattered. The nuclear family is no longer dominant. Divorce has lost its stigma. People are marrying later and having fewer children. A growing number of adults are choosing to remain single. More and more couples are living together without benefit of marriage. Gays are coming out of the closet in increasing numbers. And so on and on. As pollster Daniel Yankelovich puts it, "The rules of American life are moving us into wholly uncharted territory."

My purpose in writing this book is to examine these recent changes in American society and then see what the churches are doing about them. Do the churches know what is going on? How are they responding—if at all? To answer these questions I consulted national and interdenominational agencies to learn what the higher-ups are doing and then I have contacted individual pastors to find out whether anything has trickled down to the local parish. I have interviewed or corresponded with numerous clergy to get their reactions to these profound social changes. And I have talked with lay people who are often frustrated by the lack of sensitivity on the part of their church to their emerging needs.

One thing I have learned is that a lot is going on of an ad hoc nature. In fact, one correspondent told me that I would be better off using a mimeograph machine because my book would be out of date before it is published! So much is happening so fast. Another thing I have learned is that there is a lack of communication between the national church bodies and their local constituencies. This is unfortunate since each has so much to contribute to the other. Perhaps it will be helpful to let the right hand know what the left hand is doing. Further, I hope that my book can be useful to seminaries, which appear to be negligent in making their students aware of the challenges posed by the changing composition of local congregations.

My greatest fear is that churches—particularly in suburbia and in less-populated areas—are often unaware of what is coming down the pike with increasing velocity. And if they *are* aware, they hope it will all blow away and the good old days of simplicity and clarity will return. I have a thesis, however, which comes from experience as a college chaplain for nearly a quarter of a century. I believe that what was happening ten to fifteen years ago on the college campus— moral laxity, lack of social controls, a loss of a sense of community—is now being experienced with full force in the urban areas and will hit suburbia like a tornado before the end of the eighties.

Probably I am being too conservative. An item in the *Boston Globe* on February 10, 1982, notes that the distinction between urban and suburban is becoming increasingly blurred, with mobility and technology as the chief culprits. Meanwhile a *New York Times* report on singles in Westchester County, May 4, 1982, points out that the influx of singles is reshaping the suburbs. To be sure, critics can argue that my thesis does not apply to Big Fork, Montana or Manitowish, Wisconsin, where life and values never seem to change. But my research indicates that the rules of American life are being broken in places like Wooster, Ohio and Middlebury, Vermont. There are differences. America is vast and complex and rampant with diversity. But my advice to the still relatively sheltered is this: "Take heed. That uncharted territory may soon include you!"

Obviously a book of this length cannot encompass all the changes underway and every group affected. For example, I have not explored the *ideological* question of the role of women and minority groups. Of course they should have full equality! Each of these topics deserves a book of its own. Fortunately they are now receiving considerable coverage. But I have concentrated on individuals and groups of individuals—this includes women and minorities—who can change their identity and life-styles. Married people can choose to get divorced. Single persons can choose to remain single and even raise children. Couples can choose to live together without being married. Gays can choose to come out of the closet. And so on. I have also included some material on the handicapped; they, too, have a choice of life-styles. And I have discussed the problem of domestic violence that has such a shattering effect on the family and marriage.

This book is divided into five chapters. Chapter One summarizes the demographic changes that have taken place in the United States in recent years. One critic who read an earlier draft of this chapter suggested that I should eliminate the statistics and write it "for people whose lips move when they read." But I remain convinced that statistics are essential. The facts are complex and sometimes contradictory, and statistics are one important way to get at the truth.

Chapters Two through Four describe ways in which some national agencies of major Protestant denominations and other religious organizations are responding to emerging alternative life-styles, and summarize the programs of individual congregations that can perhaps provide models for other churches responding to social change. I consider these chapters to be the meat of the book. Addresses for all these groups and churches are included as resources for pastors and other interested persons. I have also included a bibliography of books dealing with these changes. But what should be strongly underscored is that the list of agencies, churches, and books is only suggestive and by no means exhaustive.

The final chapter contains my response to the question: What *should* the churches be doing as they move into this uncharted territory? The proposals should provoke sharp disagreement. That is fine. There are no clear-cut answers. My dream is that this book will encourage its readers to confront the issues forthrightly and then search for creative answers.

I could never have completed this project without the co-operation of scores of church leaders and followers whose responses to my queries constitute its substance. They are also the ones who convinced me that this is a project well worth doing. I want to thank my former secretary and dear friend Mary Miller for typing the manuscript and, above all, my wife, Debra, for her critical acumen and her steady encouragement to "hang in there."

Deane William Ferm
Allston, MA

One

Marriage and the Family in Turmoil

Will marriage and the family survive the 1980s? Every day it seems we see another article or newspaper story or advertisement or television program predicting the impending doom of these institutions, indeed of the very fabric of our society as we have come to know and cherish it. One fact of life is unmistakably clear: we are living in a time of rapidly changing values, a time in which traditional standards of human behavior and interpersonal relationships are being seriously challenged.

But how much of what we read and hear is really true? How much is sensational propaganda and slick advertising? After all, statistics can be found to support any thesis. As Mark Twain said, there are three kinds of lies: lies, damned lies, and statistics. I have tried in this chapter to separate fact from fiction by depending on the United States Census Bureau and other reliable prognosticators. But even they are not infallible. So this is my perception of what is happening.

1

Moral Laxity

Psychology Today in 1981 surveyed its readers, asking them how they felt about ethical decisions they might make on various important issues. The conclusions are startling, to say the least. Here are some of them.

1. A higher percentage of respondents (49 percent for men; 44 percent for women) acknowledged extramarital affairs in 1981 than in a similar survey in 1969 (40 percent for men, 36 percent for women).

2. Thirty-three percent lied to a close friend about something significant during the past year.

3. Ninety-three percent drive faster than the speed limit.

4. Sixty-seven percent cheat on exams.

5. Forty-one percent drive while drunk or under the influence of drugs.

6. Twenty-six percent would keep the extra change if a clerk gave them too much.

7. Almost 50 percent would, if their car scratched another car in a parking lot, leave the scene without reporting the accident.

8. Fifty percent knowingly give false information on their income tax return.[1]

And so on.

These figures are fairly consistent with the findings of other similar studies.[2] They clearly indicate a dramatic change in the public acceptance of moral laxity over the past twenty years. One can argue with some justification that traditional moral standards have always been broken, but one can hardly quarrel with the conclusion that moral permissiveness has become much more common and even acceptable to contemporary American society than ever before.

There are many reasons for these changing values. Increasing social and religious pluralism has led to competing value systems. The secularization of large segments of modern society has challenged time-honored religious sanctions. Expanding urbanization has led to fewer social controls and more anonymity and "do-it-yourself" life-styles. Exploding mobility has weakened familial roots. Television programs and reading materials have increasingly condoned permissiveness and violence. We have lost confidence in our governmental leadership thanks to Watergate and similar evidences of corruption condoned at the highest levels. Abject poverty and racial inequality cause the have-nots in our society to resent their exclusion from the American dream and to demand their share of the pie. And so on and so on. The reasons are legion.

It is not my purpose to analyze why this dramatic shift of values has taken place. This topic has been amply covered. But whatever the causes, there is little doubt that a new morality has emerged, characterized by public acceptance of moral laxity and by a pervasive questioning of the traditional sources of moral authority: parents, church, school, and government. These traditional moral support systems simply do not exert the same influence upon human conduct that they did in years past.

One area profoundly indicative of changing moral standards is that of sexual behavior. Each year about one million teenagers become pregnant; over 600,000 actually give birth. Out-of-wedlock births increased more than 50 percent in the 1970s. About one out of every six babies in the United States is born to an unwed mother. In New York City in 1980 more than one-third of the babies were born to unwed mothers.[3] Boston witnessed a similar pattern: 78 percent of teenage births alone were out of wedlock.[4] Fifty percent of all teens fifteen to nineteen years have had sexual intercourse. And it is clear that the era of the double sexual standard is over. Little wonder, then, that sociologist Kristin Moore laments: "There just aren't any supports for those who want to be virgins."[5]

As the traditional moral supports continue to weaken and peer-group pressure presents a bewildering array of conflicting types of behavior, young people become more and more confused about the direction and purpose of their own lives. To quote from *U.S. News and World Report:*

> Among thousands of teen-agers ... alienation and a lack of clear moral standards now prevail to the point where individual lives, families and in some cases whole communities are threatened.[6]

The report goes on to say:

> America's adolescents are growing up fast in the 80's—too fast for many to cope with adult roles. The result: Escape via drugs, suicide, crime, sex or just attempting to run away from it all.[7]

The times are indeed changing. Traditional values are crumbling. The old supports are disappearing. Moral relativism is pervasive. And the results are frightening to say the least. While many are distressed by the widespread denial of the universal values of love, integrity, justice, and human dignity, most realize that it is futile simply to try to reinvoke old standards and recreate an earlier more stable world that is quickly receding. Although that world never did reflect these universal values to any significant degree, at least it was a less complicated and confusing world for many people. But in a nation of cultural and religious pluralism one must be willing to tolerate the diversity of living patterns which have emerged as a result of a profound social revolution.

Demographic changes have transformed American society during the past twenty years. This has led to a greater variety of acceptable life-styles and living arrangements. Since the alternatives are greater, moral decisions become even more ambiguous and the difference between "right and wrong" even more blurred. Let us take a look at some of these demographic shifts of recent date and note how they lead to alternative life-styles.

Changing Demographics

The divorce rate in the United States has more than doubled during the past two decades. Although the growing divorce rate has a long history, its recent acceleration is nothing less than alarming. In the latter part of the nineteenth century one divorce occurred for every twenty-one marriages. By the beginning of the twentieth century the ratio was one out of twelve, by World War I it was one out of ten, by 1940 one out of five, by 1950 one out of four. This ratio remained constant until the 1960s when the ratio again began to decrease until by 1970 it was one out of three.[8] And the ratio continues to decline, so that it is now estimated that 40 to 50 percent—depending on which expert one consults—of the marriages taking place today will end in divorce. Although in the past decade over half of the states have adopted no-fault divorce laws, these laws seem to have had little effect on the rising divorce rate. People who want to get divorced these days are going to get divorced, no-fault or not. And they're going to get divorced in greater numbers.

It is revealing to note that the two largest metropolitan areas with the highest divorce rates in the country are in Texas: Houston and Dallas-Fort Worth. These two Texas cities have a divorce rate double that of New York City and triple that of Boston. Indeed, married couples in the West and South are more likely to get divorced than those who live in the Middle West and Northeast. Some experts have suggested that the high Texas rate can be attributed to the large number of young married couples who have moved to these areas searching in vain for a better future. We can anticipate that as mobility increases on a national scale, so, too, will the divorce rates.[9]

Traditional values and social pressures which heretofore served to stigmatize divorce have virtually disappeared. The median marriage in the United States now lasts 6.6 years before ending in divorce. Today it is almost assumed that a married couple will not spend the rest of their lives together. In a recent poll 60 percent of those interviewed said that they did not expect that most people getting married these days would stay married for life.[10] This should not be too surprising inasmuch as increasing longevity means that most married couples have to put up with each other for a much longer period of time than in previous generations. And people do change both personally and in their interpersonal relationships. Teenage marriages, as one might expect, have by far the highest incidence of divorce.

The Catholic divorce rate has doubled since 1970 and is now only three percent behind the rate for white Protestants.[11] Roman Catholics in the United States are receiving annulments of their marriage in record numbers. In 1981 there were 77 annulments for every one in 1968.[12] Andrew Cherlin notes that Catholics now resemble Protestants both in divorce rates and childbearing patterns.[13]

This is not to say that the institution of marriage is dead, but, rather, it has changed in character. Permanence is no longer one of its most prominent characteristics. And in terms of basic human values one can argue, as many do, that there is more integrity and justice to a divorce which acknowledges the death of a marriage than there is in simply holding together a relationship already devoid of dignity and love. Thus, while the increasing divorce rate may lead to greater social disintegration, divorce in itself may in many cases be an affirmation rather than a denial of basic human values.

The nuclear family (husband, wife, and children) no longer occupies the preeminent role that it held in American society for generations. This typical family now constitutes only about one-third of all households. Or to put it another way, the American nuclear family with a working father, a stay-at-home mother, and one or more children has decreased from 70 percent of all households in the 1950s to only 15 percent today! The nuclear family can no longer be considered the backbone of the American family.[14]

One of the reasons for the declining number of traditional nuclear family households is the growing tendency to marry later and have fewer children. The median age for first marriage in 1970 was 20.8 for women and 23.2 for men. By 1980 the figure was 22.1 for women and 24.6 for men. About 30 percent of first births are now to women over twenty-five years of age.

An important reason for the trend toward delayed marriage and childbearing is the growing number of women who choose to finish their education and begin their careers before they marry. The rising cost of living and the tight housing market are also factors influencing the decline in family size. During the 1970s the size of the average household declined from 3.14 to 2.75 persons. This lower birthrate combined with a lower death rate has resulted in a population older than two decades ago.

There are some indications, however, that a new "baby

boom" is beginning. Children of the earlier "baby boom" of the 1950s, now in their late twenties, have become aware of recent studies suggesting that women who delay child rearing into their thirties run the risk of being less fertile. Moreover, Andrew Cherlin argues that just as the parents of the 1950s, who were children of the Depression and victims of the social disintegration of the Second World War, turned to the more traditional patterns of early marriage and the child-rearing boom of the 1950s, so, too, may the parents of the 1980s, who were children of the social chaos of the 1960s and victims of the economic hard times of the late 1970s and early 1980s, search for stability in a return to early marriage and child rearing.[15] But this is not what George Masnick and Mary Jo Bane predict, as we shall note.

Another change affecting family patterns is the increase in the number of interfaith marriages, especially between Catholics and Protestants and particularly among young people. The present rate of Catholic intermarriage is now 40 percent and growing. Moreover, although about 72 percent of Americans now approve of such marriages compared with 63 percent in 1968 and 50 percent in 1949, statistics suggest that these marriages are more likely to end in divorce than intrafaith marriages.[16] Also, the number of interracial married couples increased by a third during the years between 1970 and 1977. Despite this increase, interracial couples still represent only about one percent of all marriages.

Another important factor is the influx of women into the labor market. Women now constitute 45 percent of the nation's work force. Since 1950 the number of families in which both spouses work has almost doubled, from 22 to 42 percent. It is not surprising that with the acceleration of the women's liberation movement in the 1970s female expectations have risen dramatically, precipitating dramatic role changes for large numbers of wives and husbands both at home and in the labor market.

Thus, the traditional role of the wife or mother in the home and the husband or father in the marketplace is rapidly becoming a thing of the past. But at the same time studies indicate that marriages in which women work outside the home have a higher divorce rate than those who do not.[17] So, although one may applaud the breakdown of the old husband-at-work wife-at-home stereotype in favor of giving each marriage partner the opportunity to share home responsibilities and develop personal and professional talents, it also creates problems as to who does what and when. Changing marital roles are a widespread problem even reaching the "Ask Beth" column in the *Boston Globe*. Beth reminds her readers of the practical implications of changing patterns in marriage:

> Marriage has become harder for everyone, because old rules no longer apply. Instead of masterly and wifely servant, couples are more likely to be partners and equals. There are no role models for this arrangement. Who pays the bills? Who cooks? Who picks out the furniture or the vacation spot? Each decision must be worked out by each couple. This lack of certainty is one reason for the rising divorce rate.[18]

Experts disagree as to how much the "modernization" of marriage and the family is a major factor in the increasing divorce rate. Andrew Greeley argues that the rising divorce rates

> are not the result of "feminism" and "the decline of the family"; they are related to poverty, perhaps the inability of poor families to cope with the heavy emotional demands of family life.[19]

But Mary Jo Bane counters this argument by noting:

> If low income were the most important explanation for divorce, however, the divorce rate should have fallen over time as family income increased. Since it did not, other factors must also be at work.

And she goes on to say:

> Marriages in which wives work tend to be somewhat less stable and report somewhat less satisfaction than marriages in which the wives keep house.[20]

Andrew Cherlin agrees, predicting that the increased participation of young women in the labor market will be the major factor in increasing divorce rates.[21]

A by-product of the growing divorce rate is the rise in the number of one-parent families. Such families headed by a woman have skyrocketed the most dramatically. In 1982 there were approximately 5,340,000 single-mother households, with more than a fifth of these mothers college educated. Even the number of single fathers raising children has doubled since 1970, to 609,000 in 1982. Put another way, single-parent families constituted 9 percent of all households in 1960; by 1980 the figure was 14 percent. Then, too, an increasing number of single parents have never married; and 75 percent of Americans now say that arrangement is morally OK.[22]

As one can surmise from the above trends, children are being reared in an atmosphere of accelerating instability. More than half of the children born in the United States now have mothers working outside the home. The largest increase has been in working mothers with preschool children, with 40 percent of these mothers in the labor market.[23] What is particularly alarming is the large and growing number of families, mostly headed by a single female parent, who live under the poverty level. Forty-five percent of infants born in the United States are destined to spend at least part of their childhood with one parent only. Single-parent families with children under eighteen years of age now number six million. In 1978, 18.1 children per thousand population under eighteen were part of a divorce. This is more than twice the rate in 1965 and triple the rate in 1955.[24] Each year for the past decade a million more children have had their family lives split apart by divorce.

The increase in the number of divorces, single-parent families, and mothers working outside the home—compounded by the growing permissiveness of contemporary society—cannot help but have an unsettling effect on children. One study suggests that children become "more cautious and tentative in establishing interpersonal relationships after divorce"; that as a result of the growing divorce rate there will be "an increasing number of unhappy children who will need the services of skilled technicians."[25]

Not all of these demographic changes, however, are linked entirely to the decreasing permanence of marriage. Another shift is represented by the booming number of single adults who choose to live alone, now almost 25 percent of American households. In the 1950s single households constituted only 11 percent; by the end of the 1980s one in three, or at the most four, households will be managed by a single person. Indeed the number of persons living alone had increased by 64 percent in the 1970s, with most of this growth occurring among divorced or never-married persons. The number of under-thirty-fivers living alone has tripled in the past decade, with women accounting for the largest proportion of this growth.[26]

Three other demographic changes merit attention. First, 30 percent of American households consist of married couples with no children, a vast increase over twenty years ago. A decrease in the importance of the nuclear family has paralleled a decrease in the importance of children as essential to a fulfilled marriage; more and more couples consider having offspring a conscious choice and no longer a foregone conclusion. Far better, say they, to have no children than unwanted ones. A childless wife is no longer considered somehow unfulfilled. Most Americans now agree that children are not essential to a successful marriage. This was not true some years ago.

Second, the number of unmarried couples living together has tripled during the past decade. For those under twenty-five years of age, the number of cohabitating couples has increased eightfold in the last ten years.[27] Although they constitute only two percent of the total number of households, all the evidence indicates that the percentage will continue to rise. In many cases such couples are not living together solely or even primarily for the purpose of having sex, as the critics would have it. Rather, they are together because they are frankly afraid of the increasing divorce rate; many of them are products themselves of broken homes. They value so much the importance of marriage that for emotional and financial reasons they are just not ready to make a long-term commitment.

Third, gays are making known their sexual preference in increasing numbers. It is estimated that 10 percent of the American population is predominantly gay. When one considers the twenty million parents and countless family members and friends of gays, it is clear that the increasingly visible gay community and its potential supporters constitute a substantial portion of American society. Numbers alone render it unlikely that the American public can continue to neglect the issue of gay human rights and dignity. To quote John Fortunato:

> To be gay and Christian . . . rejoicing in those gifts as part of the uniqueness that makes us who we are is to place ourselves on the outskirts of the community we most care about. It's beyond the realm of choice. Exile is simply where we find ourselves when we are who we are. It's most often a hard place to be.[28]

Gays are today's outcasts. In another sense so are the handicapped. In many cases the handicapped also confront alternative life-styles in that they can choose to marry and divorce, to raise children and remain single. They merit special attention here, because their condition means that they face special challenges. At least 10 percent of Americans, sometimes called the Invisible Minority, have a handicap—physical, emotional, or otherwise—and in their advancing years our older citizens often suffer additional impairments. Fortunately, federal and state laws are being strengthened to eliminate many injustices perpetrated on these human beings. But even more in need of conversion are the too often negligent or even negative attitudes of so-called nonhandicapped individuals and their callous behavior toward the handicapped. It is particularly because of this latter phenomenon that the status of the handicapped is included here.

Finally, another wholly negative development in family patterns that is clearly a result of social disintegration, psychological disruption, and economic hard times is the increase in family violence. Indeed this has become a critical problem in contemporary American society. Here are a few statements from a recent study on violence in the American family:

"If you are married, the chances are almost 1 out of 3 that your husband or wife will hit you."

"We found mothers to be the most frequent users of violence in families and sons the most common victims."

"The sons of the most violent parents have a rate of wife-beating 1000% greater than that of the sons of nonviolent parents. Generally, those who grew up in homes in which parents were violent to each other tended to be violent in their own marriages."

"One out of 3 children between the ages of 3 and 17 hit their parents each year."

"Each generation learns to be violent by being a participant in a violent family."

"Sex and money are widely believed to be the issues which cause the most trouble. But our data show that neither of these provokes the most violence. Rather, it is conflict over children which is most likely to lead to a couple of blows."

"One of the consistent findings in the study of child, wife and husband abuse was that an unwanted child is most likely to be a victim of child abuse."[29]

Other studies reveal that each year approximately 1.8 million wives are beaten by their husbands or vice versa, over one million children are physically abused each year, and nearly 20 percent of all murder victims in the United States were related to their assailants. Twenty percent of girls and 10 percent of boys will be molested during childhood, most of them by people they know.

As the discussion above indicates, marriage and the nuclear family may not be dying, but they are in the process of radical transformation and in many cases are being preempted by other life-styles. The following report of the Governor's Advisory Committee on Children and the Family for the state of Massachusetts provides an apt summary of the above remarks on recent demographic changes in America.

> Massachusetts families in 1980 differ in important respects from Massachusetts families of just 20 years ago. The total state population and the total number of families have remained essentially stable since 1960, yet:
>
> The number of divorces has tripled. More than one out of three Massachusetts' marriages now ends in divorce.

The number of single parent families jumped to 265,000 by 1976, an increase of 43%.

53% of all Massachusetts women work outside the home. In 1960 this figure stood at 38%. The largest influx into the labor market has been women with children under six.

Recorded incidents of family violence stand at an all time high. The Department of Social Services anticipates handling 25,000 reports of child abuse and neglect in 1981.

The number of live births in Massachusetts has decreased 40% since 1960. At the same time the number of births to unwed parents has increased 92%.

Taken together, these trends suggest significant changes in the structure and quality of family life in Massachusetts— challenging public policy toward children and families in a number of crucial areas.[30]

If one protests that these figures are not typical for the entire United States, that surmise is undoubtedly correct. No demographic generalizations can be made that would pertain to all areas of this country. However, my educated guess is that the Massachusetts figures are conservative in their estimates. Some sections of the country are changing even faster. No area is immune from this social transformation.

What of the Future?

These statistics present a bleak picture of marriage and the family today. So where are we going? What will the situation be like in the decade ahead of us? To be sure, no one knows for certain. As Andrew Cherlin wryly remarks: "Every change in family life since the Depression seems to have taken scholars by surprise."[31] Let us turn again to the experts and see what they have to say. In their widely acclaimed study *The Nation's Families: 1960–1990* George Masnick and Mary Jo Bane make the following predictions as to what we can anticipate for marriage and the family as we move toward 1990:[32]

The divorce rate will continue to increase. Andrew Cherlin agrees with this prediction, pointing out that "if current rates hold for the next 10 to 20 years, about half of all the marriages begun in the mid-1970s will end in divorce."[33]

The number of nuclear families will grow only slightly while other types of households will expand dramatically. Prominent among these other types of households will be married couples with no children, families headed by women, and both men and women living alone. Many individuals of both sexes now in their twenties will never marry, more than in previous generations. A large majority of adults, regardless of their age, sex, or marital status, will live alone or with children.

Young people will continue to postpone marriage and have smaller families. Almost two-thirds of the households in 1990 will be childless. By the end of this decade only about half of all husband/wife households will include children under fifteen years of age.

There will be a plurality of living arrangements. There will be no accepted norm. Living arrangements will be less structured, more fluid, and consequently less permanent. There will be much greater variety in marital and sexual experience, much more latitude for personal choice in living arrangements. Along that line Charles Lee Cole predicts that unmarried couples living together "will continue to increase and possibly become an institutionalized pattern over time."[34] Paul Glick maintains that this is an unprecedented development.[35] Judith Blake notes that with a growing number of people cohabitating, having children outside of marriage and voluntarily ending marriage, the difference between the married and unmarried state will be increasingly blurred.[36] Meanwhile homosexuals will receive greater acceptance as they become a more visible and vocal element of American society. In short, Masnick and Bane conclude:

> We project by 1990 a very diverse world of households, families and individual life histories. Households will be smaller; they will change more often. There will be more two-worker households and more households of men and women living alone than husband/wife households with one worker . . . They will create unprecedented challenges . . . that the society must be prepared to meet.[37]

Masnick and Bane assert that the number of women employed outside the home will continue to increase sharply. This addition of women to the labor force will be the biggest single factor in the changing complexion of the labor force. One can anticipate that by 1990 the percentage of women who work outside the home will equal the percentage of men. Parallel with this development will be a sharp increase in the number of husbands and wives who both work outside the home.

Finally, these changes in working patterns will have profound effects upon future methods of child rearing. As a result of either both parents working outside the home or the single parent working outside the home, there will be a major transition toward the nonparental care of children. This care will need to be supplied primarily by nonfamily sources such as the church as government funding for child care continues to dry up.

In view of the demographic changes that have taken place in the past twenty years, these predictions by Masnick and Bane do not seem extreme. Other studies corroborate their findings. Indeed their predictions seem tame alongside others. Let us note a few of these.

Letha and John Scanzoni contend that

> as more persons begin to calculate the utilities of marriage, the greater the likelihood that some of them will assess a pattern of ongoing singleness to be basically more rewarding than legal marriage.[38]

Edward Shorter insists that "the nuclear family is crumbling";[39] that the "couple-family" will be the major family in the near future. According to Shorter the couple-family will be a short-term domestic arrangement characterized by "the pattern of coming together, revelling for a few years in intense intimacy, then breaking apart again."[40] E. Mavis Hetherington and his associates maintain that children who are reared in families headed by a single female parent have a greater chance for social and emotional maladjustments than children raised in nuclear families.[41] Lucille Duberman foresees a dramatic increase in sexual permissiveness. She predicts that a new norm will dominate the sexual relationships of the future: "Permissiveness with affection, although not necessarily leading to marriage." She also expects an increased social acceptance of sex outside of marriage and asserts: ". . . the family of the future will be a reconstituted family. People will practice serial monogamy and children will take the presence of stepkin for granted."[42]

Here are some more predictions. Amitai Etzioni wryly predicts that ". . . the United States will run out of families after it runs out of oil,"[43] that "according to my calculations, if the present rate of increase in divorce and single households continues to accelerate as it did for the last ten years, by mid-1990 not one American family will be left."[44] Margaret Mead advocated what she calls individual marriage "in which young men and women can live together in a sexual relationship and learn what it is to be married, without the notion of permanence."[45] According to Ronald Mazur, the exclusive marital relationship "hallowed by the theological concept of fidelity" is actually "a culturally approved mass neurosis."[46]

We may legitimately disagree with some of these extreme statements. As Andrew Cherlin reminds us, the experts are often wrong. And they do disagree with one another. But we can hardly argue with the basic contention that major demographic changes are underway in contemporary American society which have and will continue to have profound effects on the social order and, in particular, for our concern, on marriage and the family. Cherlin summarizes the challenge that we face:

> What does it mean for people's lives and for the institution of the family when one out of two recent marriages is projected to end in divorce, when one of six women is likely to be still unmarried at age thirty, when a growing number of couples live together without marrying, when about one-third of all young adults can expect to find themselves in a remarriage following a divorce?[47]

The two major questions that we face are: first, do we recognize and accept the reality of these changes; and second, what are we going to do about it? Clearly the churches face a major responsibility in seeking answers to these two funda-mental problems. Whether and how the churches answer them will determine the influence they will have on the future of American society. Their decisions will not be easy, but their frank confrontation of these issues is both vital and urgent.

•Two

The Churches Respond

Most mainline Protestant churches are in serious trouble these days. Membership continues to drop. The 1981 *Yearbook of American and Canadian Churches,* an annual publication of the National Council of Churches, summarizes the decline that occurred in 1979 for most of the major Protestant churches, a trend that has continued since the early 1960s. Only the conservative churches are growing.

Indeed since 1966 the percentage of Protestants in the United States dropped eight percent while the percentage of adults who claim no religious affiliation rose by six percent. Why the decline in church participation? Robert Gribbon of the Alban Institute answers:

> The widely reported decline in the membership of some churches has come from a failure to attract or hold new young members rather than from any massive deterioration by older members. Decline in church participation has been greatest among the affluent and educated young. Denominations that have drawn their membership most heavily from the educated and affluent groups have lost the most. The available research indicates that on a national basis the decline in church

participation is best accounted for by a widespread value shift, rather than any particular practices or problems within the affected denominations.[1]

In general, the churches have failed to comprehend, much less confront creatively, the pervasive shift of values and the widespread demographic changes transforming American society. If they persist in neglecting the needs of their members and potential members who must cope with these developments on a day-to-day basis, the churches will face a steady drop in affiliation and attendance. To be sure, they can continue as "the faithful remnant," holding on for dear life to the faith and values of the past, but they must face the reality that quite possibly their numbers will continue to dwindle. For the churches to ignore the radical social revolution now underway and continue to gear their programs almost exclusively to the traditional nuclear family which today constitutes but fifteen percent of American households is to court disaster.

Letters received from ministers and lay people during the course of my research betray the crisis now underway in the churches. One national church executive of the United Church of Christ writes: "Few churches have come to grips with what these changes mean." An American Baptist national executive lamented that a positive response to demographic changes "is *not* taking place in very many congregations." The head of Parish Ministries for the American Baptist Churches of Massachusetts claimed that only one Baptist church in the state has a ministry with young adults. A Methodist minister, a pioneer in developing a ministry for singles and divorced persons, recently left the professional ministry partly out of disillusionment. He wrote:

> I do not see the main-line church organizations—like Methodists—having any real interest in a significant single ministry. Most of the work I did in my decade in the ministry I financed personally. Today I still do not see any good examples of singles work happening in the Methodist church.

A San Francisco church executive reported on the hazards of trying to cope with the present changes.

> People are scrambling for survival, both in terms of retaining in the worshipping community the kind of kinship ties for which family has been traditionally responsible, and in terms of congregational viability . . . There is a great deal of despair; there are many frustrated pastors, some of whom clearly burn out themselves after several years, and there is some necessary floundering along the way to making new models work.

Ministers and lay people seem bewildered. Either they ignore these social changes altogether or they acknowledge them, hoping and praying that they will go away. "Twenty-eight out of the last thirty weddings I have performed," exclaimed one minister, "have shown by the addresses they give on their marriage certificate that these couples are already living together. That's against what my church teaches." Another minister noted: "The liturgy of my church is filled with familial images that favor the nuclear family. Yet two-thirds of my congregation are single." "My minister keeps preaching about the permanence of marriage," said a divorced woman sadly. "He makes me feel so guilty." A minister admitted that he had recently baptized the infant child of a lesbian who had been voluntarily impregnated by a male friend. The "father" of the infant at the baptismal ceremony was in fact the mother's female lover! The clergyman considered it quite proper to baptize this infant, but questioned the implications of the incident for the future of marriage and the family. And a man who has made known his gay preference stated: "I'm accepted for who I am at work and in the bars, but not in my church. There I am made to feel an outsider."

One churchgoer who is single has written an article, "The Invisible Single," relating her dissatisfaction with her church:

> A single college-age person who lives with parents is not listed in our parish directory despite constant church attendance. This attitude does not seem to extend to singles whose spouses are dead. They are respectable, having fulfilled the Church's expectations of them. To some extent those who are divorced have also "failed" in their life's duty of marrying. When creative divorce classes began in this area, married people raised an outcry despite reports from divorcees who said the classes helped them cope with their new situation . . . Some years ago

our parish started a Couples' Club. As an afterthought, the Club also invited singles. I never did go, feeling unwelcome as an afterthought ... Remember that a plain single Person started Christianity, assisted by other plain singles.[2]

One individual reflected upon a prayer he had heard in a Sunday morning service:

We pray, Heavenly Father, that you will look down with pity upon the destitute, the homeless, the single and the widowed ... How would you feel if you were one of the more than 48 million singles in America listening to a prayer like that?[3]

Another person expressed her disappointment with her church in these words:

There's a young adult group in my church and I'm fairly active in that. They are very nice people. But I don't think I'm going to meet anyone there. Everyone is too good. The ones that aren't married are very, very Christian. The Lord's will is everything. And I just can't take a lot of that.[4]

One Methodist minister said that he began to understand the needs of those who lived alone when he was transferred from a suburban church whose congregation was predominantly nuclear families to an urban parish composed largely of singles. In his suburban church after-service coffee hours were polite and perfunctory; after all, the families were anxious to get home for Sunday dinner. But in the urban setting the singles stayed on and on at the social hour; they had no real homes to return to. They returned to their own lonesome selves! Surely there is a clue here for the church. What singles want most of all are acceptance and companionship. If they cannot find them in the church, they will seek them elsewhere.

And what about the divorced? The church may be the last bastion upholding the old stigma against divorce. Little wonder, then, that many divorced persons remain in the closet as much as they can or go to another church where their former friends cannot judge them or, more likely, leave the church to find acceptance and companionship elsewhere. And the same can be said for the single parent, *and* the unmarried couple, *and* the gay, *and* so on and on.

Carl Dudley puts his finger on the problem when he writes:

> In a negative way, main-line church members are vigorous in their reactions against any perceived threat to the nuclear family. Since abortion, divorce, homosexuality, and ERA are often seen as undermining the nuclear family, these issues are emotionally opposed by many church members. The most threatening issues that have attracted the attention of the main-line churches are not the broad political, social, and economic causes, but the more intimate challenges which imply changes in traditional sex relationships or the development of non-nuclear family life-styles.[5]

As Dudley suggests, the question of alternative life-styles and the changing family structure is no mere peripheral concern for the churches. Dean Hoge and David Rosen echo Dudley's statement in their study *Understanding Church Growth and Declined: 1950–1978.* Hoge and Rosen contend that for most people religious commitments are strongly associated with family and sexual matters, including the questions of premarital and extramarital sex, homosexuality, abortion, divorce, and pornography. Thus they conclude that:

> persons favoring alternative life-styles, sexual experimentation, and related cultural innovations, tend to participate less in churches than others.[6]

In short, persons with alternative life-styles do not feel welcome in the church!

So what are the churches doing about it? This chapter provides a summary of the responses of both national church bodies and individual churches with distinctive pilot projects in specific areas. But let me quickly point out that no comprehensive survey is possible. The demographic changes are taking place so swiftly that most reponses on both national and local levels are of an ad hoc nature, a response to a particular situation or need that might not work somewhere else or at a later time. We seem to be living in a time of instant issues and instant solutions that carry little hope for permanence. One needs to learn to roll with the punches and not expect easy and permanent answers. The minister quoted above is exactly right: "There is some necessary floundering along the way to making new models work." The value of this study is to indicate how some churches and church bodies have sought to meet the problems of swirling social change.

This chapter has another purpose as well. In my interviews and correspondence I have noticed that there is little contact between the local church and the national church agencies. Somewhere along the way the lines of communication have broken down. This is unfortunate since the national agencies are for the most part struggling with the problems caused by demographic changes and are beginning to produce important documents which local churches would do well to study. Let us examine a few concerned associations that are offering creative responses to the changing family structure and the emergence of alternative life-styles. Since the survey is only illustrative and not exhaustive, I have included addresses, so that readers can themselves inquire about various programs sponsored by these organizations.

- NATIONAL COUNCIL OF CHURCHES
  Office of Family Ministries and Human Sexuality
  475 Riverside Drive
  New York, NY 10115

The National Council of Churches, the coordinating body for the main-line Protestant denominations, has attempted through its literature and conferences to keep its constituencies aware of the sweeping social changes affecting American society, especially those related to family and marriage patterns. One of the emphases for the NCC's 1982–1984 period is "Individuals and Families in Human Community." Its purpose is stated in these words:

> To encompass the needs of everyone for relationships of depth and enduring value, to foster and advocate ways to strengthen families, and to proclaim the meaning of membership in the household of faith within God's "extended family."

For the next several years (1983–1988) the NCC's Commission on Family Ministries and Human Sexuality Committee for Cooperative, Long-Range Planning in Ecumenical Family Ministries will support special programs on strengthening families, on justice and families, and on violence and families. In 1982 the NCC developed a policy statement on families which summarized recent changes in family life. Some of the data we noted in Chapter One is underscored in this study: The increasing divorce rate, nonmarital living arrangements, the decline of family size and birthrates, the increase in the number of single adults living alone, wives and mothers employed outside the home, the growing incidence of premarital sex, and so on. This statement explicitly disavows the traditional views that "the only acceptable form of Christian family is the nuclear family" and that "the Christian family has a distinctive authority locus in the husband and father."

This document in its response to social changes seeks a biblical understanding of the emerging family. It notes:

> It is relatively clear that many are confused as to the biblical and subsequently theological messages about family. The critical issue here is the hermeneutical process. Some strongly believe that biblical statements speak directly to all situations across time. Others, equally as strongly, believe that the statements must be considered in the context in which they were spoken and/or written.

This document points out that in the Old Testament authority in the family resided in the male, monogamy was not specifically recommended nor polygamy condemned, the male had the easiest time in initiating divorce, intermarriage with non-Jews was usually forbidden, and children were considered a sign of God's blessing on the marriage. In the New Testament monogamous marriage becomes the norm and the notion of family extends into both blood and nonblood relationships. But the voluntary single state is also upheld as testified by Jesus' own life. Divorce is strongly discouraged and the presence of children in a marriage important but not essential. Undergirding all these relationships, as in Judaism, is the conviction of *covenant,* that somehow God is the bonding of all human relationships.

But what of today when demographic changes have shattered the above biblical models? How can the Bible help us now? Here the policy statement reflects the influence of liberation theology in suggesting that the Bible should not be expected to describe human relationships that remain normative for every age. Rather, the Bible encourages us to seek human relationships that liberate us from all forms of human oppression:

> One must discover oppression and enslavement, and participate in liberation. One must, in faith, seek to understand families from a New Creation perspective without being enslaved by cultural and sociological prescriptions of either the past or present.

The authority of Jesus, then, should not be seen as prescriptive, telling us what to do and how to behave in every situation and relationship, but rather as a healing and forgiving authority that is based on mutual caring.

Thus, the report maintains: "There is no one family structure which is intrinsically Christian," and persons must be viewed as individuals with their own needs and cares. Persons "have the right and responsibility to decide what relational structure best contributes to their ability to experience and enable the New Creation." Even divorce "may become a gift of grace if it moves one closer to the qualities of the gospel with healing." Singleness can also be a "symbol of the New Creation." The type of structure is secondary. What is the role of the family in this era of drastic social change?

> The overarching principle of family and the New Creation is that family is affirmed when it is a means of grace for its members to each other and beyond. Conversely, family reaches its limit at any point it deters its members' experience of the New Creation.

The document concludes:

> We call churches to ministries with families which seek to uncover and work for the elimination of all discrimination related to different forms, styles and stages of families including persons undergoing the experience of divorce.

> We call churches to ministries with families which enables all families in worship by developing liturgies which recognize

different forms, styles and stages of families including liturgies which support persons undergoing the experiences of alienation such as separation, divorce and death.

This report suggests to member churches a biblical perspective that takes alternative life-styles into account. While it upholds the single state as valid as marriage, it also encourages freedom of choice with respect to having children and views divorce in some instances as a means of grace and healing. Above all it recognizes and respects the integrity and rights of the individual. The report does not take a stand on premarital sexual relationships, cohabitating unmarried couples, or gay rights. The final approved document should be available early in 1983.

Thus, publications of the National Council of Churches have encouraged a flexible attitude toward emerging alternative life-styles. Along with most of its member churches, it believes that all human beings—regardless of sexual preference—should be given their full civil rights. The Governing Board of the NCC:

1. reiterates the Christian conviction that all persons are entitled to full civil rights and equal protection and to the pastoral concern of the church;

2. urges its member churches and their constituencies to work to ensure the enactment of legislation at the national, state, and local levels that would guarantee the civil rights of all persons without regard to their affectional or sexual preferences; and

3. asks the General Secretary to request the appropriate units of the Council to gather for the Board's information work already done or in process in the communions on this subject and to explore the most effective ways of relating the theological insights of the churches on the effects of discrimination and prejudice on the lives of homosexual persons in the community and the churches.

Therefore, in keeping with the high value placed on human rights and irrespective of any moral judgment on sexual orientation or practice, the National Council of Churches strongly urges the enactment of and/or amendment to present legislation to assure every person his/her full civil rights in all societal areas including employment, housing, public service, and federally assisted opportunities.

The National Council of Churches has had a special interest in ministry to young adults. The Department of Education for Christian Life and Mission publishes a regular newsletter, *Journeys of the New Apostles,* which assists local churches in the development of a meaningful ministry with young adults. The first issue, which appeared in spring 1980, announced its goal to "share the good news about young adults in and around the churches." Fourteen denominations with a concern for "the diversity of young adults, their diverse lifestyles" cooperate in this publication. The September 1981 issue contained an article by a gay divorced father.

In July 1982 the Office of Family Ministries published a third edition of *A Compilation of Protestant Denominational Statements on Family and Sexuality.* This document, representing twenty different denominations, is a highly useful summary of views on such issues as family, marriage, divorce, single persons, human sexuality, homosexuality, and gender roles.

- THE LUTHERAN CHURCH IN AMERICA
  Division for Parish Services
  2900 Queen Lane
  Philadelphia, PA 19129

The Lutheran Church in America has a specialized ministry for young adults and publishes a regular monthly newsletter, *Ministries With Young Adults.* The LCA has held a series of consultations with singles in different parts of the country. These singles have asserted that they prefer not to be set apart from the total congregation even though they have special needs to be met. The LCA has collected a number of resources on singles ministry which is available for distribution. *Ministries With Young Adults* emphasizes that many LCA congregations—particularly those in urban areas—are discovering that they have a predominance of single members, but that many of the congregations are paying little attention to the needs of these people. One of their church executives explained: "A lot of singles in cities are from somewhere else and need a community. And there are many empty churches. The energy and resources among singles in the city could help to rebuild the church." A recent newsletter encourages congregations to survey their constituencies to ascertain what are the interests of singles. "The best way to find out is to ask them directly." A step-by-step survey guideline is included. Reviews of recent books on the single life are included in each issue. A poll of congregations in the Virginia Synod disclosed that:

> In congregations with successful young adult ministry and programming, involvement occurs in at least three areas: educational, social, and service. These successful congregations tend to attract and integrate increasing numbers of young adults. Those not providing opportunities for this age group lose the young adults they may already have.

Although the Lutheran Church in America has taken the traditional position of the church with respect to homosexuality—"love the sinner, but hate the sin"—some members of the church hierarchy have been unusually sympathetic to the plight of homosexuals. A case in point is Bishop Herbert Chilstrom of the Minnesota Synod of the LCA. In his "A Pastoral Letter: The Church and the Homosexual Person" he includes these words:

> In my judgment, the sexual orientation of a homosexual person should be as incidental for his or her membership as that of a heterosexual person. As we would exclude from membership the immoral heterosexual person, so we should exclude the immoral homosexual person—but neither without the offer of pastoral care. As we would accept the Christ-confessing and moral heterosexual person, so we should accept the Christ-confessing and moral homosexual person.

I realize that some pastors cannot now—and probably never will—accept the idea that one can be Christ-confessing and a practicing homosexual person at the same time. I don't ask that you change your view. I only ask that you be patient, considerate and understanding when other pastors choose to be more open on this matter.

However, Bishop Chilstrom does not believe that "an avowed, practicing homosexual person" should be ordained to the ministry although he would ordain a celibate homosexual.

- THE AMERICAN LUTHERAN CHURCH
  Division for Life and Mission in the Congregation
  422 South Fifth Street
  Minneaplis, MN 55415

The American Lutheran Church has published extensive material on Young Adult/Singles Ministry Resources. This material underscores the varied needs of young adults: some are still tied to their families; some want to pioneer in new and independent life-styles; some live in isolated environments such as college, the military, and apartment complexes; some are divorced; and so on. Many of these individuals have lost contact with the church. Hence, certain kinds of specialized ministries are needed to make the church more appealing to this age group. They require help in both religious and moral issues, in problems related to leaving home and to divorce, in career counseling, in finding a stable environment for healthy human relationships, and in financial and educational guidance.

The American Lutheran Church publishes *Open Spaces,* a quarterly dialogue between the church and young adults which seeks a closer rapport between the church and this age group. Suggestions are made as to how to reach out to single parents, how to conduct retreats and small group discussions, how to minister to multifamily housing and to the disabled. On this latter point *Open Spaces* also shows an unusual sensitivity to the needs of the handicapped and how the so-called "nonhandicapped" must have their consciousnesses raised. As one disabled person put it:

Stairs, heavy doors, and classes that don't have textbooks available in Braille are not big problems for the disabled. The big problems are those nondisabled persons who judge according to appearance, reject what they do not understand, and fail to respect those persons who are different from themselves. This is what cripples the disabled and ties their stomachs into knots.

In 1980 the Tenth General Convention of the American Lutheran Church adopted a statement, "Human Sexuality and Sexual Behavior," which reflects the traditional church view. The legal and civil rights of the homosexual should be affirmed.

> Christians need to be more understanding and more sensitive to life as experienced by those who are homosexual . . . Persons who do not practice their homosexual erotic preference do not violate our understanding of Christian sexual behavior . . . The Church regards the practice of homosexual erotic behavior as contrary to God's intent for his children. It rejects the contention that homosexual behavior is simply another form of sexual bahavior equally valid with the dominant male/female pattern.

• LUTHERAN CHURCH—MISSOURI SYNOD
Board of Parish Education
3558 South Jefferson Avenue
St. Louis, MO 63118

The Missouri Synod Lutheran Church has family-life consultants in each of its thirty-eight North American districts. It claims a special concern for the problems of young adults and has circulated to its congregations a paper on "Young Adults: A Meaningful Ministry" to foster an awareness of the concerns of this age group in individual congregations. It notes that over 80 percent of young adults live in urban settings, that in Minneapolis alone "21 out of 30 residents are between the ages of 18 and 28." Other brochures issued by the Missouri Synod suggest an expanded notion of family beyond the nuclear type to include single parents and other single adults living alone. One gives forty-three suggestions to strengthen a ministry to singles including such advice as:

Be careful in what you say to and about singles. Singleness is not a deficient state . . . Offer divorced persons the same care and forgiveness you offer all people . . . Encourage intergenerational fellowship among all the members of the parish, married and single, young and old . . . Keep in touch with the latest literature on single and young adult ministry . . . Check out the possibilities for organizing a singles or young adult group in your congregation or community . . . Be sure the prayers used in public worship reflect the needs and terminology of singles as well as families . . . Don't try to find a marriage partner for every single person you know.

Like the ALC, the Missouri Synod literature exhibits a particular concern for the handicapped; it has published "Our Parish Partnership with Disabled Persons," which stresses the fact that disabled people are unique individuals with the same need to be loved as everyone else. The disadvantaged have special needs depending on their special handicap, whether it be learning disability, speech impairment, physical impairment, cerebral palsy, mental retardation, or whatever. It is important that church members understand these circumstances and how to deal with them, for "when a congregation, by design or default, excludes a disabled person, that congregation fails to function as Christ's church and adds to the difficult burden the disabled person must bear."

Suggestions for helping the handicapped include providing the physically disabled with easy access to the church building, special worship materials for the visually impaired, amplification devices for the hard of hearing—including a "signer" to interpret the worship service for the deaf and using visual materials for those who have difficulty understanding spoken messages. In short, the pamphlet asks:

Are we including the disabled and their families in all areas of congregational life? Are we using all of the people resources available to us? Are we finding out what new resources are available? Are we including or excluding people from certain areas of congregational life . . . there is no separate church for disabled persons. We are one flock that follows a single Shepherd.

The Missouri Synod has also taken a stand with respect to sexuality. In 1981 the Commission on Theology and Church Relations published a report entitled "Human Sexuality: A Theological Perspective," which reaffirmed its traditional position on such topics as marriage, divorce, and homosexuality.

> Marriage is the lifelong union of one man and one woman entered into by mutual consent . . . By its very nature masturbation separates sexual satisfaction from the giving and receiving of sexual intercourse in the marital union and is symptomatic of the tendency of human beings to turn in upon themselves for the satisfaction of their desires . . . A childless couple may sorrow greatly at their inability to bear children . . . we do well to share their sorrow . . . fornication is the only grounds for divorce . . . Generally a pastor who has been divorced, except in cases of unchastity or desertion on the part of his wife, ought not to remain in office nor be reinstated in the office of pastor . . . (In marriage) the Christian husband will therefore understand that the position of headship has been entrusted to him for the exercise of sacrificial love toward his wife . . . It must be said that a predisposition toward homosexuality is the result of the disordering, corrupting effect of the fall into sin, just as also the predisposition toward any sin is symptomatic of original sin.

- THE CHRISTIAN CHURCH (Disciples of Christ)
  Division of Homeland Ministries
  222 South Downey Avenue, P. O. Box 1986
  Indianapolis, IN 46206

The Christian Church has developed resources related to the problems of demographic changes for use by local churches. One is "Family Network Mailing," a collection of articles and reprints dealing with alternative life-styles. A recent packet included articles on "One Job, Two Careers" (husbands and wives who share jobs), "Sexuality Education for All Ages," "Lonely Widows Learn to Cope in Las Vegas," "When Friends Are Divorced," and "The Multi-Level Family of God" (stressing the importance of singles ministry). Most of these articles are reprints from other magazines. The packet is up-to-date and distributed three times a year.

Most significant is the study packet on "Homosexuality and the Church." It is designed for congregations that wish to learn more about homosexuality and the issues involved in being a homosexual. It includes a wide-ranging discussion of various attitudes and assumptions about homosexuality and an annotated bibliography for those who wish to learn more. The Task Force on Family Life and Human Sexuality concluded after eighteen months of study:

> There is no evidence that persons whose sexual orientation is to those of the same sex constitute a greater danger or threat to society than any other persons . . . [and that] the church's teaching and failure to teach about homosexuality has often relied on "a questionable use of Scripture and on a relatively unexamined cultural inheritance."

Also important is the Task Force's statement: "Homosexuality is not an 'illness' which can be 'cured'; homosexuality is not caused by parents and families of the individuals."

The Christian Church cooperates with other denominations in a program called Joint Educational Development which concentrates on tasks considered crucial for the future of church education. One by-product is the pamphlet "Liberating Words, Images, and Actions. Guidelines to Alleviate Stereotyping." This pamphlet seeks to help church members avoid "ageist, sexist and racial stereotypes" and to ask for "equal time for female, male, androgynous, and nongender metaphors for God." It suggests a wider, more inclusive concept of the family and the need to educate churches to be sensitive to this new vision of family life.

> Varieties of family structure and life should be assumed and directly shown through stories and other means. Some examples are: one-parent families; extended families; employed mothers engaged in a variety of occupations and, in some instances, making use of day-care centers; non-employed mothers who are interesting people engaged in creative homemaking and community activities; fathers taking care of babies and doing domestic chores. The aim should be to portray the variety that actually exists and also to show that the qualities of good parenthood are not necessarily tied to any one pattern of family life.

- AMERICAN BAPTIST CHURCH
  Department of Educational Planning Services
  Valley Force, PA 19481

The American Baptist Church has to date done little to prepare its churches to meet the problems created by changing demographics. While there is no denominational program specifically designed for singles, single parents, and others, occasional pamphlets issued by the denomination focus on some of these groups. One such pamphlet is *Living as a Single Parent* (Valley Forge, PA: Judson Press). The December 1981 issue of the *Baptist Leader* focused on the family with one article on single parenthood. Also, a series of publications on remarriage and the family will be coming out in the near future.

The American Baptist Higher Education Team has funded a resource manual, "Congregations, Students and Young Adults," written by Robert Gribbon of the Alban Institute. This so-called "action information book" in intended for churches that are involved in a ministry to young adults and commuter students. It seeks to answer the question: "What forms does ministry need to take for those individuals who are in transition, searching, forming an identity, and finding a place for themselves in our society?" Included in this material is a study course to assist older lay people in understanding the specific needs of these young adults.

This study guide notes that, due to the baby-boom years (1947–1957), there are more young adults now, the period of young adulthood has lengthened, more young adults are postponing marriage, and more are residing longer in their own local communities. This period of life is marked by a willingness to experiment with new life-styles, a critical attitude toward traditional values, a close identity with one's peer groups and a reluctance to make permanent commitments to marriage, occupation, or locality. After all, as the saying goes, one is only young once! This is a difficult time for young people and deserves utmost sensitivity on the part of older adults. Gribbon suggests the model of the good uncle:

The uncle can care for the other, but not demand obedience. He can treat the other as a person in his own right, but not demand a full reciprocity in the relationship ... The good uncle is a model of care between generations—it is a model of one who is concerned for the other, and who lets the other go. It is a model of one who operates out of an integrity that is not afraid of questions.

Young adulthood is like the time of blossoming ... If we do not encourage the full development of the individual in the young adult years, there will be no productive years.

- SOUTHERN BAPTIST CONVENTION
  Family Ministry Department
  127 Ninth Avenue, North
  Nashville, TN 37234

The Southern Baptist Convention continues its strong emphasis on family life and includes in this concept a ministry to senior adults and singles. Beginning in 1981 it has set aside a Single-Adult Sunday, a day when regular Sunday activities will underscore this growing segment of the church. It also has developed special training kits for programs to assist singles and divorced persons to gain self-acceptance and group acceptance in their family and church. The monthly magazine *Christian Single* contains snappy up-beat articles that cover topics from exercising and scuba diving to more informative articles dealing with singles in government, how to improve interpersonal relationships, and how to avoid temptation and self-pity. This magazine also lists resources for singles and single-parent families and notices of religious retreats being held for single persons.

The SBC publishes other monthly magazines dealing with special groups: *Home Life,* a Christian family magazine; *Living with Teenagers,* for parents of teenagers; *Living with Children*; and *Living with Preschoolers.* It also distributes articles from other publications which treat themes germane to our study. Such articles include "Why Wait Till Marriage?", "Can a Good Case Be Made for Sexual Purity before Marriage?", "Homosexuality in Christian Perspective," "The Church's Ministry to Gay People and Their Families," "Why Is Sex

Sinful?", "What about Living Together?", and "The Bible and Sexuality." The answers are that sex should be confined within marriage at all costs and that homosexuality is a sin, both answers grounded in biblical verses.

- UNITED CHURCH OF CHRIST
  Board for Homeland Ministries
  132 West 31st Street
  New York, NY 10001

The United Church of Christ, acknowledging that more than one-third of the adult population is single, has developed an extensive program for ministry to singles. One of its resources is a planning packet which gives ideas on how to start a singles group, how to move from information to program, and examples of what is happening in various individual churches.

The UCC also has what it calls a "family life suitcase" which it distributes to individual churches. This suitcase contains material on family life including an entire issue of the *Journal of Current Social Issues* devoted to the theme "Is the Family Dead?" which notes the decrease in importance of the nuclear family and the increase of alternative life-styles. The emphasis is on intergenerational activities; i.e., the need to involve mixed age groups in common learning experiences. The UCC in 1981 selected family life as a priority on a national scale for the next three years. It urges members to

enlist all parts of the church, as witnesses for Christ and humanity, in study and action to the end that
- all families be ministered to creatively;
- all persons, regardless of their family patterns, be affirmed and supported in the life of the church, manifesting our unity as a family in Christ;
- networks of support be built to encourage and celebrate faithfulness, love, and justice for all family members;
- social, economic, and political conditions and policies which create family stress be analyzed and addressed.

Thirty conferences of the UCC have already accepted the family-life priority and over one-third of them are in the process of developing family-life task forces.

The United Church Press has produced a planning guide, "The Church's Growing Edge: Single Adults," sponsored by the interdenominational Joint Educational Development partnership. This document seeks to assist member churches in developing successful ministries with single adults. It provides detailed information on how to organize a singles program, from gathering data to determine if there are enough interested singles to discovering areas in which interests and needs seem most intense. Included is a singles survey form suggesting how to gather the information necesary to plan and organize a singles group. The document also discusses types of singles ministries—recreation, supportive, study, service. The underlying philosophy is that "Singleness is not a disease for which marriage is the cure. Singleness is a growing life-style ... Nothing in scripture teaches that marriage is preferred."

A recent study by the United Church Board for Homeland Ministries, "Looking Over Our Shoulders: Recent Social and Religious Changes Affecting Church Life in the Middle West," made some predictions about the church in the 1980s. Some of the conclusions are:

> Work with young adults needs a good deal more attention than it is receiving in most of our churches ... Current evidence that the "baby boom generation" will return to church involvement is at best mixed. Some will return but it now appears that the number who will return is dwarfed by the number who will not ... We need to place ministries with young adults toward the top of our evangelism agenda ... Effective outreach to new urban residents will challenge our present homogeneity. Effective urban evangelism will require significant adaptation to new racial and ethnic groups and to persons whose life-styles are frequently at variance with those of our present members. The cities can be a land of opportunity for the mainline churches.

Additional evidence for the fact that the UCC is deeply concerned about the future of the family in all its variety is that the May 1982 issue of *A.D.*, the official magazine of the denomination, had as its theme "The American Family Today." It included articles on "The Myth of The American Family"

("The notion of the steady, unchanging American family may be true as a myth, but it is false as history."), "Life Beyond Divorce," and "The Second Time Around."

- UNITED PRESBYTERIAN CHURCH U.S.A.
  Youth and Young Adult Program
  475 Riverside Drive
  New York, NY 10015

In 1979 the Unit of Ministries with the Laity of the United Presbyterian Church U.S.A. initiated an eighteen-month project to study the most effective ways of ministering to young adults (ages eighteen through thirty-five). As a result of this study several Guidelines for Ministry were developed. These Guidelines are well worth quoting in part.

Guidelines for Ministry

1. *For many young adults, early adulthood is necesarily an age for stepping away from institutions, including the church . . .*
Therefore: Church outreach to young adults must combine innovation and pastoral caring—and realize that even *that* may be rebuffed.

2. *Given the tendency for many young adults to leave the church, it may be that the space enclosed by the four walls of the church is not the best arena for ministry.* The church must do more to take its ministry into the marketplace; the marketplace of ideas as well as the marketplace of shops and stores . . .
Therefore: The church should be clear about the need to enunciate its Christian message in the secular world. The church must realize that the best place to bring the message of Jesus Christ may be in storefronts, community centers, and housing complexes.

3. *Today's young adults are the leaders of tomorrow's church— but not necessarily of our local congregation.* Frustrating as it may be for a congregation which has invested energy, love, time, talent, and money into outreach to young adults, there may be little or no immediate payback in the local congregation. One reason is that some seeds bear fruit more slowly

than others, and when the young adult blossoms, he or she already may have moved on to a new location, occupation, or vocation.

Therefore: Standard investment principles may not be the best tool for evaluating church growth.

4. *For many young adults, the church has been on the "wrong" side of many issues (political, theological, liturgical, economic, life-style, spiritual).* On the one hand, the church (or organized religion) fails to meet the needs of people, is apathetic and uninspired, is too materialistic, is too preoccupied with money, is out of date, is out of touch with reality, is not reaching enough young people, is too hypocritical, is too smug, is not true to faith, and is not adequately digging into the real problems facing humankind.

Therefore: The challenge of ministry to young adults is to encourage discussion of these criticisms. Church people should acknowledge where the church has been in the wrong and work to interpret to young adults the areas in which the church has been trying to be true to its mission.

5. *Church people should recognize that while many young adults may be antichurch, they are not necessarily antireligion . . .*

Therefore: In ministering with young adults, it is helpful to look at ministry as comprising four mutually reinforcing types of love. As a first step, ministry with young adults is to attempt to bring about a sense of internal wholeness and self-worth that is crucial before a person can love others. The next step is to help people move into a self-giving love. The third progression is to develop love which takes the form of a caring community. Finally, ministry should strive to foster the love in which the caring community ministers to others outside itself. *Through this means the church can show that it is an institution that cares about the emotional and spiritual growth of young adults.*

To reinforce these Guidelines the project has published two monographs: *Stories of Significant Young Adult Ministries* and *More Stories.* The first publication tells the stories of thirty-seven significant young adult ministries in the United Presbyterian Church. The sequel includes stories from churches of mostly black, Native American, or Hispanic membership.

We shall refer to a few of these accounts subsequently. Also available is supplementary material explaining how to use *Stories of Significant Young Adult Ministries* and related resources.

Two other studies by the UPUSA are of particular importance for our purpose. One is entitled "That All May Enter. Responding to the Concerns of the Handicapped." This study, a policy statement of the General Assembly of the UPUSA, urges that

> planning for new church buildings and major renovations to existing church buildings shall take into consideration the needs of the handicapped members of our society, in order that all may enter into our fellowship.

The Program Agency is also directed to "begin exploring possible ministries with the physically, emotionally, and developmentally disabled and to share these ideas with congregations and judicatories." The other study, also a policy statement by the General Assembly, is entitled "The Church and Homosexuality." This document urges that

> the church must turn from its fear and hatred to move toward the homosexual community in love and to welcome homosexual inquirers to its congregations. It should free them to be candid about their identity and convictions . . . Homosexual persons who sincerely affirm "Jesus Christ is my Lord and Savior" and "I intend to be his disciple, to obey his word and to show his love" should not be excluded from membership.

After this promising beginning, however, the statement regresses:

> Our present understanding of God's will precludes the ordination of persons who do not repent of homosexual practice . . . On the basis of our understanding that the practice of homosexuality is a sin, we are concerned that homosexual believers and the observing should not be left in doubt about the church's mind on this issue.

But this action should have no effect on homosexual ministers already ordained! As Martin Marty notes:

... a little hypocrisy is what the Presbyterians seem to have settled for on the homosexual issue ... Neither the PCUS nor the UPCUSA is willing to ordain an avowed, practicing homosexual. Both maintain that the Bible forbids it ... Avowed, practicing homosexuals may be members of the church ... But they should not be ordained.[7]

As we have noted, Presbyterians are not alone in this hypocrisy.

• PRESBYTERIAN CHURCH U.S.
341 Ponce de Leon, N.E.
Atlanta, GA 30308

Perhaps the most significant publication of the Presbyterian Church U.S. is *1/3 of Our Congregations: The Singles.* This brochure is used widely by many denominations. It includes a survey form to test the effectiveness of congregations in their present ministry to young adults, including how members feel about singles. Further, there are statements made by singles concerning how they feel about the church's attitude toward them and a list of suggestions the congregation could use to improve its ministry to these singles. This involves the following: Work with singles to find ways either to form special groups for them or to incorporate them into the mainstream of the church's life—whichever they want. Be careful to avoid exclusive familial language and assumptions. Think of particular ways to minister to people at the time of divorce or death of a spouse. Provide a lending library of resources dealing with singleness: its problems, potentials, and challenges. Give singles ministry a high priority and lots of attention for one year to find out the needs. Make the congregation aware of singles. The brochure also lists recent books on singles, single parents, and divorced persons.

• UNITARIAN UNIVERSALIST ASSOCIATION
25 Beacon Street
Boston, MA 02108

It appears that the Unitarian Universalist Association is the only denomination that issues a special information packet on lesbian and gay concerns. It is a compilation of recent articles and pamphlets. Included are "Gay Questions/ Straight Answers," "Answers to a Parent's Questions about Homosexuality," "Parents of Gays Speak Out!", and "What Jesus Christ Said about Homosexuality" (the "text" of the last is a blank page). The UUA has its own national office of Lesbian and Gay Concerns, created in 1973. As early as 1971 the UUA General Assembly adopted a resolution that included the statement: "Private consensual behavior between persons over the age of consent shall be the business only of those persons and not subject to legal regulations."

In 1980, concerned that some UUA member societies were not accepting gay ministerial candidates because of their sexual orientation, the UUA General Assembly asked their Department of Ministerial and Congregational Services "to lend full assistance in the settlement of qualified openly gay, lesbian, and bisexual religious leaders."

The Office of Gay Concerns claims to be the only officially sponsored voice for gay liberation among the Protestant denominations.

- THE UNITED CHURCH OF CANADA
  Division of Mission in Canada
  85 St. Clair Avenue East
  Toronto, Ontario M4T 1M8

The United Church of Canada has produced among other things a book-length mimeographed study guide entitled *Marriage Today. An Exploration of Man/Woman Relationship and of Marriage.* Although this is not an official statement of the Church of Canada, it does carry the approval of the Church's Division of Mission. Its purpose is

> to look at changing patterns in marriage and the alternatives to traditional marriage now developing in our society, and to consider what needs to be done in helping people understand the directions of these changes, deal with their impact on their own lives and, hopefully, make some contribution to the shaping of future society in this area.

This study is sensitive and nonjudgmental in helping to understand alternative life-styles and what seem to be their strengths and weaknesses. The writers affirm as important values the worth of the human person, the need for friendship and loving relationships, and the urgency to alleviate the hurt in human relationships. But how these values are fulfilled can be a matter of personal preference, whether it be as a single person, in monogamous or open marriage, in a gay union, or in any other kind of relationship. The heart of healthy interpersonal relationships is intimacy, that is, "the process of discovering another—and yourself—to be lovable, trustworthy, stimulating, joyous, beautiful." This should be the heart of marriage—and for some persons

> in a strong open-marriage relationship the couple might consciously decide not to be possessive of each other's person or body, freely giving the mate the freedom to develop other relationships to significant levels of intimacy, not excluding genital sex.

What is so impressive about this study is its candor and its honest struggle with the issues. It recognizes that there are no easy answers, that to be human is to be uncertain. The report concludes:

> We live in a world of uncertainty. Many of our decisions must be made tentatively, even when they are based on the very best knowledge we have at our disposal. Clearcut rights and wrongs are harder to find than in days past. Instead, we have to make our decisions from among qualified rights and even qualified wrongs. Sometimes, subsequent events prove our decisions to have been good ones; often they prove to have been undesirable or mistaken. But decide we must lest . . . we die through indecision. We pray for more light, but we must also follow the light we have.

• THE UNITED METHODIST CHURCH
Board of Global Ministries
475 Riverside Drive
New York, NY 10115

Perhaps the most distinctive program of the United Methodist Church with respect to special ministries is its concern for the handicapped. In 1981, the International Year of Disabled Persons, UMC developed printed materials to assist local congregations to "respond to the concerns of those persons with mental, physical and/or psychologically handicapping conditions, including their families." A special pamphlet, "Study Guide on the Church and Persons with Handicapping Conditions," gives a biblical and historical perspective and concludes:

> We call upon the United Methodist Church to hear the voice of its Lord and open all of its doors in welcome to those persons with mental, physical and/or psychologically handicapping conditions, including their families, and actively seek out these persons for whom and with whom Jesus lived, ministered, and died.

In 1983 the emphasis of the UMC will be on Women and Health and in 1984 on Total Family Wholeness: Spiritual, Physical, Emotional Well-Being of Intergenerational Interaction in the Home. The Board of Discipleship is in the process of assembling a packet of materials for Singles Ministries. It should be available by the end of 1982.

• THE EPISCOPAL CHURCH
815 Second Avenue
New York, NY 10017

The Episcopal Church began in 1978 to publish a quarterly newsletter, *Sound the Call,* promoting young adult activities in the local parish. It reports on young adult programs in existence across the country and lists resources that are available for local churches. It has also helped to coordinate national services on "Intimacy in Young Adulthood." The purpose of *Sound the Call* is to help "to provide a community of caring and loving people who are committed and dedicated to the Good News."

- CHURCH OF THE NAZARENE
  Department of Adult Ministries
  6401 The Paseo
  Kansas City, MO 64131

The Adult Ministries Division of the Church of the Nazarene has an extensive list of materials and programs designed for such groups as the formerly married, singles, single parents, and even preretirees. Defining adults as "over 23," the Nazarene Church notes that:

> During the 50 years of adulthood, people go through as many changes in life as they do in the previous 23. Because physical changes are more apparent than spiritual, psychological, and sociological, we tend to overlook the importance of ministering to the needs of adults until the physical changes of old age become apparent.

The material offered to local congregations is extensive and has been particularly strong in a ministry to single adults. In this area both resources and articles are offered to help implement a singles ministry. In one such article the question "Why Should the Church of the Nazarene Become Involved in Ministry to Single Adults?", is answered by the author, Harold Ivan Smith, as follows:

> The reality is either we minister to them or someone else will. Many single adults have grown impatient. As they become aware of ministry in other fellowships it creates a hunger for ministry.
>
> They are ours—Nazarenes. So why should we be hesitant to minister to our own people? We would not consider allowing other denominations or independent churches to minister to our children. Many single adults have cut their teeth in our churches and in our camps and in our colleges. They have every right to expect a loving, redemptive response from us.
>
> Our emphasis on forgiveness and personal standards. We expect a high standard in our programs and ministry.

Our emphasis upon the Holy Spirit. Single adults quickly learn the inadequacy of their own resources. Programs and seminars on positive single living may be helpful but an over-emphasis on self-reliance shortchanges the single adult. The Holy Spirit has come as the enabler to strengthen the single adult to live a celebrative, redemptive, victorious life.

Our emphasis on involvement—service . . . We are a partici-pant fellowship. Attend one Sunday and you can be a member of our Sunday school. Everyone can be used. There are plenty of opportunities for service.

Our emphasis on fellowship. "Shining lights on Sunday nights" means an active fellowship. A variety of experiences for spiritual enrichment and development are offered. These provide the emersion of the single adult into the lifestream of the church.

Realistically, there are those "prodigal sons." There are too many who have expected too much from the church or given up too easily. Many sat back and waited to be served. Some felt abandoned; some have tasted of the enemy's opportunities.

We are being called to develop a program that is Christ-centered and which reaches out to individuals and warmly draws them into a loving fellowship. We are being called to minister to those who are "near" and those who are "far away," in Paul's words.

Not every congregation can have a formal single-adult ministry—but every congregation can minister to the single adult within the fellowship. Jesus spoke of doing simple things in his name, i.e., "the cup of cold water."

We are not going into ministry to single adults because it is a fad or because First Baptist Church has a program and we'd better start one. We initiate a single-adult ministry because there is a need—and the need does not seem to diminish.

Jesus understood singleness—He never married. Therefore His Church must reach out to those who are single and proclaim the good news: "For in him dwells all the fullness of the Godhead bodily, and you are complete in him" (Colossians 2:10).

- REFORMED CHURCH IN AMERICA
  Office of Family Life
  Box 803
  Orange City, IA 51041

The Reformed Church in America has begun to alert its congregations to the diversity of households within the church. The Christian Action Commission recently passed the following recommendations:

> To direct and encourage all assemblies and congregations to consider the many varied family units within our concern, to exclude none or over-emphasize any, to seek a wider ministry to all the family units and living arrangements within our church mission.

> To call on congregations to examine their corporate lives to seek out ways in which a limited definition of "family" has resulted in the exclusion of peoples from the ministry of the church.

A national church executive pointed out that the RCA is trying to become much more inclusive and to "help churches think in terms of households rather than the traditional nuclear family." The RCA publishes a quarterly pamphlet *RCAgenda*. A recent issue is entitled "Homes in the Household of Faith." This issue points out the diversity of family households. "We use the plural, not the singular, as a way of keeping in mind the many different kinds of homelife and living arrangements that people (yes, including Christian people) now have." The report goes on to say:

> When we mention "family" in a church setting, we must make clear to the "atypical" eighty-five percent that they're as mainstream as almost anyone else . . . We are now heading toward new patterns and traditions that balance individual well-being with the well-being of the family as an institution . . . It is also vital that the local church become a support group—a caring community—for persons struggling with these sorts of difficult but not impossible tasks. Often churches are faulted for following instead of leading society. In this case, however, the church may be the one institution in our society uniquely suited to helping people aim for—and achieve—new family traditions.

•Three

Pilot Projects: Significant Local Ministries

Most of the individual churches that have sought to respond to demographic changes have done so in terms of a ministry to singles. We shall take a look at some of these programs that seem particularly significant and have weathered the test of time. But we shall also include a few ministries to groups other than singles. Once again it should be emphasized that our survey is not comprehensive. Similar church programs of equal worth could have been cited; my primary purpose is to indicate the kinds of programs that are now in existence. Once again I have included addresses, so that readers can use this chapter as a resource and consult with congregations that have programs suited to their own particular constituency.

• FIRST CHRISTIAN CHURCH
1221 Park Avenue
P. O. Box 952
Burlington, IA 52601

First Christian Church (Disciples of Christ) has had an active singles program since 1975. After trying for several years to organize a posthigh-20s fellowship with no lasting success, several singles organized "The Christian Brethrenaires" to provide a setting where middle-aged singles could make new friends with those of the same age bracket who had similar problems and needs. What started out as a once a month get-together has now become a weekly event and includes those from age thirty to retirement age.

The CB's are loosely organized with no elected officers nor set term of office. A person remains as chairperson, for example, as long as he/she wants and then the executive board chooses a successor. There are no requirements for membership nor any dues. Everyone is invited and a free-will offering is taken at the "regular" meeting the first Saturday of the month when the minimal business matters are conducted. The CB's are ecumenical in character and are sponsored by the area Association of Churches. The ecumenical setting allows for more variety in terms of persons, ideas, and interests.

The Brethrenaires are basically a social group, not an alternate church. They seek to provide interaction and security for kindred spirits. But the fellowship has attracted individuals who felt left out in their own church and who often, because of their association with the Brethrenaires, were then able to return to their churches no longer feeling like "odd numbers." The organization also maintains a library of "how to cope" books for individuals who are struggling through personal crises. The CB's have also influenced churches in the area to change their exclusive emphasis on families and couples to a more universal term for the *adult* age group.

The Brethrenaires has had such successful staying power over the years that, in response to many requests, it has developed a two-page suggestion sheet. Included are the following recommendations:

1. Make it ecumenical. You need a broader base than just one church. Besides, your singles probably already know each other.

2. Determine the age group most logical, where need seems the greatest. Senior Citizen groups take care of the older people here; we have a need for a younger group. Ages can be broken down to fit your need.

3. Find a strong leader of the same age with a good reputation—and *single*! One with discussion-group leadership experience is ideal. Must like people and handle them well.

4. Get the backing of the local church or ministerial association. This is very important if you're going ecumenical. People need that security, it says this group is OK. The Christian atmosphere is a necessity.

5. From those ministers ask for a list of singles of the proper age group in their congregations so those singles may be contacted personally. Send each one a letter asking them to attend an organizational meeting. State its purpose, give details as to where and when it is meeting.

6. Find a comfortable meeting place. You'll need recreational space in addition to attractive meeting room. The church we use has a game room with Ping Pong and bumper pool which really helps. You'll need tables and chairs for the meetings at which you serve food.

7. At the first meeting, which 35 attended here, we just did a welcome then we went around introducing ourselves, giving occupations, etc. We numbered off in groups of 4 and were given some discussion questions, such as "What do you find the most difficult about being single?" and "Have you experienced discrimination toward singles, where and in what way?" Make up your own questions. We then appointed a spokesperson for each group and shared some of the replies. It was like opening the flood gates! We had coffee, a period of visiting, and decided to continue meeting on a regular basis and set the time. We were off and running. That was in January 1975. We have 100 or so on our mailing list, which constantly changes, average 35 at events. . . .

9. We decided very early there would be a devotion at the start of our regular meeting (first Saturday night of the month). We have a meditation at the monthly breakfast, ask grace before eating at all events. This lets anyone coming know this is a Christian group and we've never had any trouble with "swingers." We share our faith but do not debate it since we come from such varied backgrounds.

10. About finances. We take a free-will offering at the meeting first Saturday night of the month which is the only meeting where we have a business session, committee reports, etc. There are not many expenses but we do rent films occasionally, pay for the meat at some parties, etc. We have also adopted a family for Christmas baskets, etc., asked members to bring canned goods and gift items for that, bought the rest.

11. Your group needs will determine how many chairpersons and committees you need. Ours have changed with time. We are very informal in our organization and in our meetings.

12. We have a telephone committee sometimes used for special events but have very good newspaper coverage announcing dates of meetings, etc. Also everyone gets a copy of the next month's calendar at the previous meeting. We use a sign-up sheet for new members so we have addresses and telephone numbers of everyone.

13. Your natural leaders will surface very fast. We do not designate specific terms of office, simply replacing a chairman when one wants to be. This method works for us, you may wish to be more structured.

14. About resource materials. Every Christian bookstore and publishing house now has fine books on divorce, single parenting, widowhood, etc. You're lucky—the world is just discovering that over ⅓ of adults over age 18 are single; the church is just beginning to respond to that large group of people. Watch the film catalogues, TV programs for discussion after, etc. Pickings were slim in 1975!

15. SOLO magazine is an interdenominational publication for Christian singles which you should subscribe to, both as a resource for program material and for ideas . . .

16. Vary your programs, not all of ours are serious with discussion groups or speakers. In fact they are hard to find unless

you live in a big city with lots of possibilities. Eating together brings out the biggest crowd—eating alone is lonely! We've had everything from barbershop quartets to a lawyer speaking on taxes. A good program chairman and his/her committee worry with all this! We have a separate recreation chairperson who arranges the mid-month party which may be a tour, eating at a restaurant, a potluck and cards after, etc.

17. Our name, "The Christian Brethrenaires," was thought up by a Baptist fellow and accepted as a compromise at the time. We have come to see it as most appropriate and we'll keep it—the CB's for short.

18. This is a good evangelism tool—we have church members who came to our church because they got to know some of our members through the Brethrenaires. We now have a Singles Sunday School Class made up of people who were not S.S. attenders previously. Their material is not "singles" related—they select their own books for discussion, etc.

• FIRST BAPTIST CHURCH
1401 12th Street, Box 4309
Modesto, CA 95352

The First Baptist Church in Modesto, California, has a minister on the staff with a specific responsibility for single adults. This church has a decidedly conservative theological orientation, with the singles group having its beginnings in Bible study and a Singles Sunday School class. Over the years the group has grown rapidly, so that the Sunday morning classes are now split into age groups such as twenties, thirties, forties, and fifties, with the entire group meeting together Sunday evening. This singles ministry uses married couples to add stability to their leadership. As their singles minister puts it:

The Singles leadership exit cycle can keep a group in a continued state of instability. As the key people in leadership marry, often there are not enough singles to assume leadership responsibilities and confidence is lost as well as positive direction and continuity.

It is important that the leadership couple have a real love for single adults; their age is not so important. That there is a bias in favor of the married state is clear from their minister's remark about the importance of the married couple: "They will be the living model for singles to be learning from to see how a Christian marriage really works." Single leadership in the group is not elected by the group but chosen by the couple. All leaders must be church members since nonmembers feel no responsibility to spiritual authority and so often cop out when facing a difficult challenge. Above all, "Becoming skilled in learning the Word of God is key in the development and spiritual maturity of your group."

The singles ministry in this church differs markedly from the first one we encountered. The first one is decidedly social, ecumenical, and deliberately low key in theological concerns. The latter is conservative, theologically, with a strong biblical basis and an equally strong tie to the local church.

The First Baptist Church also carries on other special programs geared to the special needs of singles. A recent series of Saturday evening programs for single parents presented such topics as "Single Parenting," "Losing Custody," "Being a Step-parent" and "The Single Mother: To Work or Not to Work?" These special programs are designed for a wider appeal beyond the church itself and are usually intended for singles, single parents, and divorced.

- WESTMINSTER PRESBYTERIAN CHURCH
  2110 Sheridan Boulevard
  Lincoln, NB 68502

The singles ministry in Westminster Presbyterian Church began in 1977 for the purpose of enabling people to *grow* through a divorce (GTD) rather than *go* through a divorce. People who are single for whatever reason are encouraged to participate in a regular Saturday evening program. A second group, Another Way (AW), is designed primarily for those who are widowed or never married. Both groups participate in a monthly newsletter, *First Person, Singular,* which lists the activities of both groups and includes personal items telling of the accomplishments of various members. Both groups meet together for potluck supper on Saturday evenings and then separate for their own programs. The stress is on small groups, with individuals encouraged to participate regularly in a series of carefully designed sessions lasting over a period of ten months. Although activities of a more recreational and social nature are also encouraged, the leadership team—consisting of seven individuals—is responsible only for the designed sessions. This leadership is taken seriously by the individuals who covenant with one another as follows:

1. I will *commit myself to living in community* with the others of the Ministry Group.

Note: "Living in community" includes such things as mutual support, accountability, acceptance where you are, being vulnerable, confronting where you are from where I am, life-sharing, gift-evoking, planning for ministry, group prayer. Meetings of the Ministry Group will include all of these and others, though not necessarily in the same meeting.

2. I will *attend the weekly meetings* of the Singles Ministry Group.

3. I will *use my personal gifts regularly* in one or more ministries of the Ministry Group.

4. I will *use my material assets generously* with 10% of my income (a tithe) being the minimum I will give in any year. (Persons not currently at a 10%-giving level may have one year of grace to move up to that level so as not to shock their budget too severely.)

5. I will *be open to God daily for my growth,* choosing one or more of the following avenues:

a. quiet/meditation	d. dreams
b. prayer	e. Scripture
c. journaling	f. worship

6. I will *be intentional about my personal growth and training for ministry* by participating in workshops, institutes, and events at Westminster and elsewhere.

7. I will *participate in the parish life* of a Christian church.

• ASBURY UNITED METHODIST CHURCH
5838 South Sheridan
Tulsa, OK 74145

The Single Adult Ministry of Asbury United Methodist Church
has as its purpose

> to give each adult a positive self-image of themselves as God
> created them ... [with] an emphasis on personal caring rela-
> tionships which bring single adults into the fullness of life and
> ministry God has for them.

This varied program includes Friday evening sessions for
widowed persons, an Around Thirties Single group, Singles
Sunday Nites, Bible study for singles, movies, and so on. A
bimonthly newsletter describes the activities. Special one- or
two-day workshops are held, two of them recently having as
their themes "Growing Through Divorce" and "Sexuality
and Singleness: Value Systems." Each year there is set aside
a "Singles Sunday" in which "singles, divorced, widowed,
and single parents" are recognized. The purpose of this special Sunday is to indicate that churches need to become better
acquainted with their single adults and that every believer,
regardless of single or marital status, should be incorporated
into the life and ministry of the church.

• GOLDEN GATE COMMUNITY
1387 Oak Street
San Francisco, CA 94117

Golden Gate Community is an urban mission project of the
Church of the Nazarene. Inaugurated in 1981, the project
presently consists of a handful of members who live as a
community and have covenanted together to create an innovative approach to the urban scene. The GGC holds regular
worship services on Wednesday evenings and Sunday morn-
ings. It seeks to provide a presence in the Haight-Ashbury
area and is organizing a street theater which will perform in
shopping malls, parks, prisons, and churches. It also extends
hospitality to other church groups that want to spend a day
in the area to note the problems an urban setting faces.

The GGC is clearly an experimental venture. The director himself admits that "most of the urban pastors I know, including myself, are frustrated and at a loss on how to deal with the marginal groups in the mobile anonymous urban environment."

- WARD PRESBYTERIAN CHURCH
  17000 Farmington Road
  Livonia, MI 48154

Ward Presbyterian Church has developed a multifaceted type of ministry for single adults called Single Point Ministries. With a strong evangelical and biblical base, the church sponsors in-depth seminars on such topics as grief, divorce recovery, single parenting, and sexuality. It has established groups for single parents, the newly married, and the widowed. Every other Friday night there is a general meeting which features speakers and entertainers in an atmosphere of warmth and acceptance. A monthly "Single Scoop" newsletter describes upcoming programs. One recent issue showed only two days in which no activities were scheduled. Included were regular programs such as bowling league, camera club, Bible study, and drama rehearsal. Special activities included a divorce-recovery workshop, a spring retreat weekend, a personal development course, an evening of testimony by a converted prostitute and her husband, a single-parent workshop, and still another workshop on "How to Survive the Loss of a Love." The minister to single adults stresses the importance of lay leadership that is carefully cultivated and developed. Indeed, as the minister himself says, "A singles ministry can be tremendously self-supporting. Singles are willing to give once they are challenged."

Single Point Ministries in the fall of 1982 sponsored the national Single Adult Leadership Congress, held at Ward Presbyterian Church. This congress tackled such problems as:

- what the difference between a club and a ministry really is
- how to begin a singles ministry

- how to apply the Word to single adult lives
- how to organize your leadership core
- how to attract men to singles ministry

- MIDDLETON OUTREACH MINISTRY
  7325 Hubbard Avenue
  Middleton, WI 53562

The Middleton Outreach Ministry began as an attempt by St. Luke's Lutheran Church to meet the spiritual needs of the 60 percent of the community who live in multifamily apartment housing. The associate pastor of the church moved with his family into one of the apartment complexes to begin a low-key ministry. MOM has now become an ecumenical venture supported by the local Catholic, Episcopal, and Community churches. It publishes a newsletter, *The Good Neighbor,* which lists the services and activities available in the apartment complexes and in the greater community. The rationale for this ministry is that "when people don't come to church, the church must come to the people." Apartment dwellers have the same needs as everyone else—and some of these needs, such as loneliness, are compounded as "shut-ins" have so little contact with the outside world. MOM offers counseling, programs, and opportunities for church participation. MOM cooperated with several other similar ministries in convening the national Apartment Ministry Conference held in Overland Park, Kansas, in 1980.

- GETHSEMANE LUTHERAN CHURCH
  11560 S.E. Market Street
  Portland, OR 97216

For the last five years Gethsemane Lutheran Church has sponsored a special apartment ministry. Recognizing the large number of apartment dwellers in Portland, this church believes it has a responsibility to reach and serve these people. Since the problem of accessibility is so great, special steps have to be taken to alleviate it. The most important is to develop a friendly working relationship with the managers of the apartment complexes. The attitude of those particular key persons can make or break a successful ministry, for it determines the degree and ease of access. The minister offers his services for crisis counseling and for marriage and parenting problems. Lay members who live in the apartments serve as advisers and as advocates of the ministry to other apartment dwellers. In the apartment complex itself the minister offers brief courses on "parenting," "stress management," and Bible study. The church also provides a list of public resources and services for every resident.

- TRINITY EPISCOPAL CHURCH
  Copley Square
  Boston, MA 02116

Trinity Church in the heart of Boston believes in the "small group" approach. These groups, run entirely by lay people, deal with basic human needs and self-destruct after six weeks. Several of the programs run concurrently on Sunday evenings preceded by a worship service and supper for the entire group. Snappy brochures describe the programs, which in recent months have included such topics as "positively single," "formerly marrieds," "the predicament of work," and "coping with urban life." Trinity Church attracts many divorced and single Episcopalian parents from the suburbs who find in that church the support groups they need and a certain preferred anonymity in which they can make known their hurts and dreams. Trinity also sponsors concerts and art displays as a service to the larger community.

- GARDEN GROVE COMMUNITY CHURCH
  12141 Lewis Street
  Garden Grove, CA 92640

Garden Grove Community Church has an extensive program for single adults called *Positive Christian Singles.* Within this umbrella organization are four autonomous groups: Pacesetters (20s), Innovators (30s), Motivators (40s) and Lamplighters (50s and over). A wide range of activities is covered throughout the week, with Sunday worship and Bible study the focus. The administrator for PCS offers the following advice to other churches seeking to launch a singles group:

1. Make an announcement from the pulpit inviting all singles to fill out a card indicating interest in forming a singles group. Include this card in that morning's bulletin. Drop it in the collection plate. *Important:* Define singles from the pulpit as being divorced, widowed, and never-married adults.

2. Respond to the cards with invitations to the first meeting. Serve coffee and cake. Chat; get to know each other; determine the purpose of forming the singles group. Discuss goals. (The following has been useful to us, and may serve as a guideline for your discussion.)

   a. Spiritual Fellowship
- Bible-study—weeknight
- Sunday School—a specific place and a male teacher, preferably single. Teacher that can relate to singles.
- Sunday Service together after Sunday School class.
- Talk-It-Over (TIO)—weeknights. As this is one of the more important things we do, I include a section on it later.

   b. Social Life
- Brunch together Sunday afternoons
- Sunday afternoon sports, picnic, excursion
- Weekend activities: barbecue, tennis, volleyball, rap sessions over coffee and sandwiches, potlucks, game nights, taco bust, skating, bike rides, concerts, out-to-the-movies together, etc.
- Activities with the kids: picnics, swim parties, snow trip, beach trip, zoo trip, etc.
- Church-related social events. Singles have much to offer and contribute—don't isolate them.

The administrator also suggests the following ideas:

1. Growth potential as a group; growth as individuals. Growth through understanding and acceptance.

2. Include other congregations in the singles activities (i.e., community involvement).

3. Christians vs. non-Christians. (Note: every Christian was once a non-Christian. We at GGCC have found the singles group to be a subtle, gentle, loving way of bringing non-Christian, hurting, lonely people to the Lord.)

4. Leadership. This is important. Those who are willing and capable should be utilized and much appreciated.

5. Publicity—both within the group and in the community. Ours includes: a monthly calendar listing all functions, which is available to every single and to any inquiring visitor or single person in the community who requests it; pamphlets; church bulletins; community newspapers, etc.

6. Age grouping. You may find that within the singles it would be well to form smaller components based on age/interest factors. Be lenient here, and only "group down" if it seems good for your composite situations. In any case, keep your identity as singles—and all members of that larger group.

7. Acceptance. Be aware of criticism one to another. Most of our singles here at GGCC are divorced and have gone through experiences that have been hurtful beyond belief. They want and need to be accepted for who they are, where they are, and to be loved and helped to heal and grow as individuals.

8. Visitors need to feel particularly welcome. We have a policy of filling out a card, introducing them during Sunday School or Talk-It-Over, following up with a card or letter to their home. Free brunch for first-timers may be in order.

9. Child care supplied and paid for by the church singles group is worth considering, since there will be many who cannot otherwise attend any functions besides Sunday School.

10. Singles have particular needs, hurts, fears, joys. They need to have time to get together with other single adults to talk about their feelings, ideas, struggles, aspirations. Our Talk-It-Over addresses this need. This should be a time of warmth, drawing together, and personal growth. It is not a time of Scripture study, but rather a time of "self-study," although Christian topics and principles make good topics for discussion.

We set up our TIO thus: Every Tuesday evening, 7:30 to 9:30; general gathering with songs, announcements, introductions of new folks, etc. for ¼ hour. At about 8:00 we break into small groups of 8–10 people. A group leader (enabler) was the topic for the evening's discussion, which has been determined by the person or persons in charge of the TIO. Discussion lasts until 9:30 and varies within each group depending on the needs of the group and the enabler's guidance of the discussion. (Our enablers are drawn from volunteers who are Christians, good listeners, comfortable in a group, and sensitive to people's needs and group patterns. As your TIO solidifies you may wish to initiate a program of enabler training. We have chosen to do so, and have developed materials that we can send to you upon request.)

Typical discussion topics have included: loneliness, sharing, breaking down communication gaps, forgiveness, jealousy, self-image, surviving as a single, thinking remarriage, self-improvement goals, fruits of the spirit, what do I want in a companion?, love, values as a single adult, single parenthood. (The list of possibilities is endless.) One Tuesday night each month we invite a guest speaker (Christian counselor, psychologist, etc.) to speak to the entire group on some growth-related topic. We always share coffee after our TIO, either at the church or at a local home or restaurant. Child care is provided on Tuesdays and paid for by the group.

- ## FIRST UNITED METHODIST CHURCH
  1411 Broadway
  Lubbock, TX 79401

First United Methodist Church has had a significant singles ministry called BREAKTHRU for a number of years. A description of its history and development is well worth quoting.

> BREAKTHRU was begun in March, 1979, as a mission outreach of First United Church in Lubbock, Texas, to the singles community of the greater metropolitan area of this "Hub City." Some estimates place the singles population at 30,000, with 12,000 of those being divorced persons. BREAKTHRU is advertised as an interdenominational, citywide program, and seeks to be complementary to already-established ministries within local church units, of whatever denomination they may be. BREAKTHRU does not seek to estrange a person from a previous church commitment or a "way" of experiencing the religious life. About 85% of the participants are not related to the programs of First Methodist Church. It often does not appear to be "churchy" in its programs or activities. It is more aligned with the bush-beaters (God seeks out all persons) than it is with the gate-guarders (keep the program doctrinally "clean").

The philosophical undergirding of BREAKTHRU rests upon the dual concepts of the HOLISTIC and the RELATIONAL approach to understanding human nature. It is holistic in that it attempts to minister to the "total" person. BREAKTHRU recognizes that heterogeneity is one of the important characteristics of those it serves and that individual needs and histories are quite varied. It is relational in that is understands itself to be a catalyst for interpersonal communication, assisting each person to be "Christ" to his brother.

The conceptual has been made concrete in a model that has been successful in several larger communities where there is a large singles population. The program revolves around a weekly Tuesday night meeting that is located in the Fellowship Hall of First Methodist Church. The format of the evening is: 6:30 supper, 7:30 program, 8:30 informal recreation, and 9:30 GROUPDATE. This model allows persons to be reached on the physical, mental, and emotional levels in one evening, in one setting.

Supper is a hot meal consisting of salad, main meat entree, one vegetable, bread, iced tea or coffee, and dessert. The charge for the meal is $2. Two persons active in the BREAKTHRU ministry have assumed the main responsibility for the menu planning, food purchasing, and cooking and serving of the meal. Sometimes the meat dish or the cooking of the pies is "farmed out" to the church hostess who charges BREAKTHRU only actual costs of the ingredients. Therefore there are no labor costs involved in the meal and it is possible to serve a quality meal at a reasonable cost. The church does have a complete kitchen and refrigeration capabilities.

Supper is important for two reasons. One is simply that one can get a tasty, hot meal without either the personal investment of time and energy in the kitchen or without high cost. The other reason is the fellowship that emerges from sitting across the table from one another. Many men have said that it was the good meal that attracted them for they tend to cook little for themselves. Others have mentioned that they come because it gives them a chance to put a few names and faces together in an informal setting. It also gives the "core group" a chance to catch up on the events of the past week in their lives. Supper signals that BREAKTHRU is a person-oriented program and assists in a smooth transition into the program period. It has been our experience that those who do not come to supper, but to the program only, are not as easily integrated into the activities of the organization and that they often experience a coldness that those coming to supper never express.

The program hour creates an educational forum that is directed to the single life-style and/or current events that touch all citizens. Highly qualified speakers from throughout the professional community are invited to speak on a topic appropriate to their training. Speakers are not paid; few persons contacted refuse the invitation. It is our practice to commit speakers three months ahead of their coming: in a year's period, only one speaker has backed out. Films, musical groups, and special presentations are also used, but most programs are one-person-presenter occasions. Because of the size of the group (usually averages 180 per night), seating is arranged in horse-shoe type rows with the speaker to the front, center. A microphone is necessary. Audiovisual aids are present when requested. A time at the end of the program is left for a question-and-answer period. Sometimes, with the help of a highly skilled speaker who is trained in group dynamics, the larger group is broken up into 10 or 12 smaller units. Our experience has been, however, that the noise level of verbal interchange is excessively high and that some persons are highly uncomfortable in such verbal situations.

The informal recreation period takes place in another area of the church and consists of Ping-Pong, pool, bridge, shuffleboard, general conversation, and milling around the coffee pot and cookie tray. This period gives persons an opportunity to dialogue informally with the speaker if they desire, or to participate in recreational activities, or to meet new people. Sometimes dance lessons have been offered in an adjoining room. About 50% of those who attend the program stay for recreation. There are no organized mixers and no formal ending to the period. First Methodist Church does not have gymnasium facilities and that is the reason that no more strenuous activities are held.

GROUPDATE arose out of the cultural uniqueness of west Texas. Many of the persons who came to BREAKTHRU in its early months, and still do, were avid Country-Western dancers. They began to gather informally after the recreation period and go together to a local dance hall. It became apparent that integrating this into the evening's activities would be advantageous and the concept of GROUPDATE was born. One of the purposes of BREAKTHRU, as stated in the early stages of planning, was to offer a noncompetitive environment in which persons could make friends and participate in enjoyable and affordable activities. The group was emphasized in GROUPDATE. Thirty, or forty, or even seventy persons would go out and meet for dancing . . . most without a formal "date." This relieved the pressure on many persons, created a protective environment, and offered another opportunity for personal interaction. This section of the Tues. program is not considered a "formal" part of the design—but a very important part. The dance locations have been expanded to include Disco and Oldies but Goodies.

The Tuesday evening program is the focus of BREAKTHRU but certainly not the only part of its outreach. Weekend activities are planned throughout the year and may include parties at apartments or in homes, bridge and game nights, volleyball challenges, biking tours, hiking events, out-of-town trips (retreats, ski trips, tour trips, trips to special sports or musical events), a tennis league. Short-term workshops are offered at various times during the year and may include support groups, dance lessons, topical study or skills development.

The mechanics of BREAKTHRU work in the following way:

Leadership
Minister with Young Adults is Coordinator and M.C. of the weekly Tuesday meeting. He consults with an Advisory Board made up of 12–15 persons representing the makeup of the group; the Board is repopulated every 6 months or so to replace those who are no longer participants. Membership on the Board is by invitation rather than by vote. There are no officers, except for a Treasurer. BREAKTHRU was designed in this manner to facilitate immediate planning and the quick implementation of a program. Initial members of the Advisory Board were singles and supportive couples from First Methodist Church. It is possible that leadership will be developed from within the group and an officer-type council established at a later time. At this point some of the stable and supportive members are quite involved in the structure of their own church's ministry (one example is that the Young Adult Coor-

dinator of the downtown Baptist church, a lay person, is a faithful and supportive participant in BREAKTHRU activities) and it has not been our desire to "plug them into" roles of equal responsibility in BREAKTHRU.

The Advisory Board meets quarterly to review the past 3 months and to look ahead to the following 3 to 6 months. Surveys are taken on Tuesday evenings about every 6 months (some more comprehensive than others) and this data is used in the planning of both activities and programs. If there are special needs, members of the Advisory Board assume leadership of task areas, which are terminated as the need is met; there are no ongoing committees. Programs are arranged by the Coordinator.

Finances
A small portion of the cash-flow needs of BREAKTHRU is available through the church budget. Baby-sitting costs are included in the budget as are utility costs and the time of the church hostess (when used) . . . The commitment of time by the Minister with Young Adults must also be seen as a financial commitment of the church. The more ongoing costs, such as publicity, mailing, office costs, activity costs, etc., are financed outside the church's budget. There are two main sources of revenue.

One of these avenues is private gifts of those who are supportive of this "newer" ministry of the church. Some funds are deposited in "designated" accounts that cannot be used for other purposes. Another avenue is the small profit made from each meal served. Through good planning, effective purchasing and the elimination of labor costs, about $.50 can be made (average) off each meal. We have found our break-even point to be 75 meals and we usually serve 120–130. This $60 a week is put in a BREAKTHRU bank account, established outside the church's treasury, and is used to "pay the bills."

Most activities, such as bus trips, are costed out so that they are totally paid for "out-of-pocket" by those going. The largeness of the group helps keep costs down, however, and only moderate $ obligations are necessary.

We have not had to resort to projects such as garage sales or bake-offs at this time, leaving BREAKTHRU great latitude in meeting future needs.

There are no dues or contributions asked of BREAKTHRU members. No contributions are made by other church groups to the BREAKTHRU treasury.

We consider BREAKTHRU to be self-sustaining.

General Purposes
As stated in various BREAKTHRU material, the purposes are:

(1) To encourage persons to accept themselves as loving persons.
(2) To help create a supportive group of singles who care for each other and who are thus enabled to "get outside" of their own problems and become sensitive to the needs of others.
(3) To create an educational forum that promotes the growth of the total person by dealing with areas of concern common to most living the single life-style.
(4) To provide a noncompetitive environment in which a single person can make new friends and participate in a wide range of enjoyable and affordable activities.
(5) To provide special short-term special interest groups such as divorce support groups, bridge lessons, weekend retreats, trips to the opera, etc.

Relationship of BREAKTHRU to the Young Adult Ministry of 1st. Methodist
Because BREAKTHRU is understood to be a mission outreach of 1st. Methodist, there was little expected "pay-off" in new church membership. There has, of course, been some spin-off in terms of persons interested in the church school and interested in membership, but this has not been the purpose of BREAKTHRU. It is much more analogous to Methodist Hospital, which is there to heal people and not to determine the level of their religious commitment. Perhaps it is a halfway house of sorts, meeting people where they are and serving as a catalyst to healing. Perhaps BREAKTHRU can point to the source of healing and direct the person to a more direct channel for the understanding of the source and a commitment to it. BREAKTHRU is included as a part of the "business" of the Commission on Education, but has a kind of "independence" unique to itself—again, perhaps, like the Boy Scout and Explorer troup.

Promotion

Because BREAKTHRU has little of a "captive audience," it must seek out persons from other sources than its own congregation (about 10–15% of those active are members of 1st. Methodist). The media is used as effectively as possible to tell the story. Newspaper articles about the nature of the group have appeared on the religion page several times and the organization is listed weekly in community happenings. We now seek to get a story in the life-styles section of the newspaper. Good public service exposure has been given BREAKTHRU by at least 5 radio stations; scripts are written and taken in person to the appropriate persons at the stations. No TV has been attempted. An unexpected return has come from early contacts made with professional counselors and psychiatrists from around the area. Many singles have been referred to BREAKTHRU by counselors who felt their client was prepared for the resocialization phase of their, usually, unexpected singleness. Agencies, such as the Family Services Agency and the Texas Tech University Counseling Center, have been most helpful also.

However, as one might expect, word of mouth is the best advertising and the most effective. Each week about 20–30 new persons visit BREAKTHRU for the first time and about 30% have learned about the organization through a friend.

Publicity to the mailing list (now 1,300) is essentially information about upcoming programs and activities in the form of announcement brochures and/or cards. No newsletter has been established because of the lack of logistical support.

Follow-up

Because of the size of the group meeting and because of the heterogeneity of the group, it is important that new persons experience as positive a welcome as possible on the first night, or they may not be motivated to return. Persons come with expectations that may or not be met and with their own built-in hesitancies. On Wednesday, after the Tuesday night meeting, a letter is sent to each visitor expressing our pleasure at their coming and it includes a coupon for $1 off their next meal. This letter is on BREAKTHRU letterhead. We also place them immediately on the mailing list. (We accomplish this by a FIRST-NIGHTER sign-up list on our SIGN-UP TABLE area, which is next to the program information area.

As new persons enter the door into the Fellowship Hall they are met and greeted, given a special name tag that identifies them, unobtrusively, and are told about the various lists on the sign-up tables. This usually leads them to sign for us, giving complete address information.)

A card file is kept on each person and as additional information is gained by various means, it is added to the 4 x 6 card. (Other means are by gathering personal information from survey sheets, from trip survey sheets, bridge sign-ups, etc.)

Summer Conference
Because BREAKTHRU understands itself to be interdenominational and city-wide, it was felt that sponsoring an area conference for singles during the summer months could accomplish several things: (1) it could communicate to the community at large that singleness is O.K., is a wholesome state, is important to the vitality of the community and is often stereotyped in ways that are unproductive to the strength of the individual and his community; (2) that it could bring individual church ministries into conversation one with another for general support and common ministry to the total singles population—a more coordinated approach than heretofore existed in Lubbock. The attendance goal is 1,000—the first undertaking of this size, ever. The target area covers all west Texas and eastern New Mexico.

Logo and Name
We live in an age of image creation and it was felt that it was important to develop a logo and name for the organization that neither used a traditional Sunday-school type name nor suggested a close organizational tie to the structure of First Methodist. The name BREAKTHRU was chosen and a logo suggesting the struggle and final breakthru of the embryonic inhabitant of the egg into the world and the life-sustaining nature of the sun was designed. Early advertisements read: BREAKTHRU to new levels of caring . . . sharing . . . coping . . . hoping . . . self-understanding . . . self-acceptance . . . decision making . . . barrier breaking. The logo is used on all publications, on stationery, and will soon be featured on T-shirts.

- **HYDE PARK COMMUNITY
  UNITED METHODIST CHURCH**
  Cincinnati, OH 45208

Hyde Park Community United Methodist Church has had a singles ministry since 1975. It has developed out of the expressed needs of the community and is open to the entire community. The greatest need has been with separated/divorced persons. Two classes of eight-weeks duration that are particularly popular are "Growing through Divorce" and "Learning to Love Again." The waiting list for these classes is so large that additional sessions are held throughout the year. Programs are offered every Sunday evening and cultural events are scheduled throughout the month. Leadership is provided by the group itself, with the church staff working in the background. This successful singles group has developed some common sense ideas for a successful singles ministry which it shares with other potential singles groups. Here are its suggestions:

1. First and foremost—we are people oriented. We practice fellowship and reaching out to others. We try to meet people where they are.

2. We give a friendly welcome to newcomers. We try to identify them and recognize them without embarrassing them. We want them to return.

3. We want people to feel safe. No hassle. We want to provide a sanctuary, a haven, and allow them the space they need. We try to provide support and acceptance.

4. We try to provide means for personal and spiritual growth.

5. We find that a mutual support system emerges from this emphasis on persons.

6. It is helpful to discuss and define the needs of your group at the outset.

7. Closely related to the needs is agreement about goals and objectives of your group. It is helpful to write down your goals and objectives and refer to them as you grow.

8. We find that singles do not have a lot of spare time. Thus, most of the offices are for a three- or six-month term. After all, no one is indispensable. Further, it keeps from "burning out" leaders.

9. It is helpful to define and structure responsibilities as needed. The structure arises out of the needs of each group.

10. It is good to delegate work to several persons. We find that maximum autonomy for each group and for each job within the group is especially effective.

11. It is rewarding to see how many talents are to be found within your own group. We suggest that you seek out these programs and leadership talents.

12. We find that programming on a 52-week per year schedule requires some imagination. Try to be aware of program resources within your group, within your church, and within your community. Local universities and public agencies are good resources.

13. We consider each single in the church as a family unit. It helps us to relate better to a couples-oriented church and increases their consciousness of us. After all, each single is a wage earner and often is a contributor to the church.

14. We are working toward greater involvement in mainstream church activities. We desire to be a part of the main body of the church.

15. Last, but not least, have fun. Plan activities, outings, and dances.

- ## ST. PAUL—REFORMATION LUTHERAN CHURCH
  100 North Oxford
  St. Paul, MN 52104

St. Paul—Reformation Lutheran Church has recently begun to develop a ministry to the gay community. Its rationale for initiating this program is important.

Statement of Need
There is an almost history-long experience of alienation and brokenness which gay and lesbian persons have experienced with society as a whole and with the church in particular. In recent years there has been an attempt on the part of the church to come to terms with the reality of the gay/lesbian experience and orientation with the result that there is, in some circles, a willingness to provide healing through God's grace and the church's ministry of the broken relationships between gay and straight persons.

There is a distinct need now to make possible a ministry to and with gay and lesbian persons within the context of a normally functioning congregation like SPR. Since this congregation has provided a spirit of openness to gay and lesbian persons over recent years it is appropriate that SPR be considered as the locus of this ministry. It is equally important that this ministry be viewed as one which will help to create an open climate among other Lutheran congregations where gay and lesbian persons can feel welcome and part of the ongoing life of the Christian community.

The specific needs which give rise to this ministry include the following:

(a) To address the brokenness experienced by lesbians and gay men as they come to understand who they are and realize the contradiction that society usually cannot or does not affirm them as persons;

(b) To address the brokenness of parents and friends of gay men and lesbians who are needing support and information as regards the gay orientation and an appropriate view of Christian faith in regard to gay persons;

(c) To address the exclusion of gay men and lesbians from full participation in the church;

(d) To address matters of fear and mis-information that clouds the issue of same-sex orientation, and of sexuality in general;

(e) To respond to the questions raised in the church about the ordination of openly gay and lesbian persons;

(f) To participate in advocacy for the civil rights of gay and lesbian persons in structures of society;

(g) To address child-custody questions for gay men and lesbians;

(h) To respond to physical assaults on lesbians and gay men;

(i) To examine the wholeness of gay and lesbian relationships.

Functions of this Ministry
As this ministry begins it is important to see its functions as open to change as we see the ministry developing, but at its inception the following emphases seem to emerge:

(1) *Pastoral Care:* relating to the human needs of gay men and lesbians and those whose lives are touched by them (family, friends). This would include counseling, worship-related activities, and inclusion in the ongoing life of this or other congregations.

(2) *Education/Consultation:* providing education and consultation in this and other Lutheran congregations in order to provide a more open climate for gay and lesbian persons, reducing the fear and apprehension of such persons by providing information and interpretation of the gay experience from a scriptural/theological perspective.

(3) *Witness and Advocacy:* providing support, intervention and encouragement to the society as a whole in order to advance a better quality of life for gay and lesbian persons. This may include addressing specific legislative issues which may arise in local, state, or national legislative structures which affect gay and lesbian persons.

Other Significant Local Ministries

As mentioned earlier, the Special Project Staff of the UPUSA under the direction of Allen Kratz has compiled two resource books, *Stories of Significant Young Adult Ministries* and *More Stories,* which summarize forty-six different stories of important young adult ministries. Kratz looks upon these stories as a map, not a detailed aerial photo, which suggests ideas that "can be *adapted* to local situations, not formulas that must be *adopted* for a 'successful' ministry." It might be helpful to look at a few of these stories.

- FIRST PRESBYTERIAN CHURCH
  302 North Dunton
  Arlington Heights, IL 60004

First Presbyterian Church in Arlington Heights, Illinois, sponsors "Time Out," a six-week series sponsored continually throughout the year to assist young adults in developing social fellowship, recreation, spiritual growth, and leadership opportunities. This church also sponsors The Community of Singles, an ecumenical ministry for singles of all ages. This group tends to attract persons who are older and who are widowed or divorced.

- FIRST PRESBYTERIAN CHURCH
  2407 Dana Street
  Berkeley, CA 94704

First Presbyterian Church in Berkeley, California, deliberately mixes single and married persons because of their shared concerns (e.g., relations, sexuality, community, finances) and to underscore for both singles and married persons their similar problems. This church does have a special concern for single parents in their need for extra support.

- FOURTH PRESBYTERIAN CHURCH
  5500 River Road
  Bethesda, MD 20016

Fourth Presbyterian Church in Bethesda, Maryland, feels a special responsibility to a large and diverse group of career single adults who flock to the nation's capital for employment. This church believes in going to where the singles are and, consequently, Sunday morning Ambassador Fellowship programs are held in a civic center and at a Ramada Inn. Said the sponsoring pastor: "If we want to reach single adults, loners, and nonchurch people, we should identify with them and make use of neutral facilities."

Weekly Bible studies are also held during the week in members' homes in Virginia, Maryland, and the District of Columbia. The pastor stresses the importance of motivating and training good leadership. What is crucial is "definite study material and good management. Too many singles groups wander aimlessly and go from one program to another."

- FOURTH PRESBYTERIAN CHURCH
  126 East Chestnut Street
  Chicago, IL 60611

Fourth Presbyterian Church in Chicago has a large singles membership: two-thirds of its congregation. Since it has such a membership, the church sponsors four single-adult groups according to age. A single person whose divorce has not been finalized is ineligible on the grounds that "being exposed to eligible singles could distract an estranged husband or wife from seeking possible reconciliation with his or her spouse." These groups run themselves informally. They emphasize the humanity of their members, not their singleness.

> Singles are people; they want the same things as married people (love, companionship). Singleness is not a holding pattern for marriage. We just encourage people to live life, not to find a mate.

- NORTHSIDE ECUMENICAL NIGHTTIME MINISTRY
  3212 North Broadway
  Chicago, IL 60657

Northside Ecumenical Nighttime Ministry is an ecumenical venture that provides a ministerial presence in bars on Chicago's North Side. The minister seeks to gain the confidence of bartenders who then make referrals to him. He sees his role as providing "a caring ministry with street people."

- FIRST PRESBYTERIAN CHURCH
  219 East Bijou Street
  Colorado Springs, CO 80903

First Presbyterian Church, Colorado Springs, has a large number of singles divided into three groups: *The Growing Edge* (21 to 35), *The Going Concern* (30 to 50), and *The New Dimension* (over 50). Growing Edge caters largely to individuals who have never married, Going Concern to persons who are divorced or separated, and New Dimension to widows and widowers. Divorce-recovery workshops are held twice a year for a period of six weeks. Topics include the stages of the divorce experience, assuming new responsibilities, and being a single parent. These workshops attract large numbers of unchurched persons. This program for divorced persons was initiated only a few years ago when a task force on single adults discovered that in 1977, for example, there were more divorces than marriages in El Paso County. As a result the congregation hired a full-time minister of single adults.

- FIRST PRESBYTERIAN CHURCH
  607 West Smith Street
  Corry, PA 16407

First Presbyterian Church in Corry has developed a program called "Time Out" that is designed for young mothers, mostly nonchurch members, who need time to themselves. Every Thursday morning they can leave their small children under professional supervision at the church. Meanwhile, the children have the opportunity to play with other children their own age.

- LAFAYETTE-ORINDA UNITED PRESBYTERIAN
  CHURCH
  49 Knox Drive
  Lafayette, CA 94549

Lafayette-Orinda Presbyerian Church believes in singles programs with an "affirming, open, nondoctrinaire tone." This openness extends even to "nonmarital relationships which are going through stress; for example, living-together arrangements." A packet with information about future programs is sent to anyone who requests it. Conferences are held on such themes as "The Single Search," "Achieving Your Potential," and "Perspectives on Being Widowed." A brochure of particular relevance is "Suddenly Single," which lists agencies and support groups in the area for the purpose of telling divorced, separated, and widowed persons where they can obtain assistance.

- **WEST HOLLYWOOD PRESBYTERIAN CHURCH**
  7350 Sunset Boulevard
  Hollywood, CA 90046

West Hollywood Presbyterian Church sponsors a Lazarus Project for gay persons. Its purpose is to integrate gay people into the life of the church. About 70 percent of the church membership is gay. A counseling service is provided for gays in the area and the church facilities are made available to other gay groups. The Lazarus Project also ministers to gays in prisons, including prison reform to curb harassment. It reaches out to the non-gay community to foster understanding and reconciliation. One recent innovation is a "road show" in which gays visit churches and other organizations to explain what it means to be gay. The Lazarus Project is unique within the UPUSA. Because of its uniqueness the minister's suggestions to other churches need to be quoted at length:

> 1. For all churches: Since you have gay people in your congregation and your community (visible or invisible to you), positive discussion and dialogue on the subject of homosexuality will enable self-acceptance for gay folk and create opportunities for openness and reconciliation among heterosexual and homosexual members of your congregation and community. Sermons, forums, church school classes all could be used to enable such a dialogue.
>
> 2. A certain amount of your church budget is given by gay people, so it would be appropriate to designate some monies for enabling special presentations (which might be advertised within your community as well as within the churches of your

presbytery). Presbytery resources also might be tapped for major conferences.

3. Your church session may wish to adopt a statement regarding the acceptance of people within your congregation as full members regardless of sexual orientation, thereby becoming a "More Light" congregation.

4. Your church staff should be encouraged to become more informed about the personal needs of gay men and lesbians and their families through reading, conferences, and continuing education.

5. Finally, your church may want to look for opportunities to follow the mandates of the 1978 General Assembly in working for civil rights and social justice for homosexual persons.

6. For churches which find themselves in the midst of gay ghettos: The 1978 General Assembly encouraged the development of ministries within the gay and lesbian community. Yet only one such ministry could be reported to the 1980 General Assembly. Your congregation may want to develop an outreach ministry similar to the Lazarus Project.

You may or may not choose to hire a part-time or full-time director of such a project. If you need financial assistance in developing the project, you could seek support from higher judicatories. This would involve writing a proposal which would need the approval and funding of your session, presbytery, synod, and the Mission Development Committee of the UPCUSA. (The latter likes to fund brand-new projects, so it is important to gain its approval before starting any project and certainly before hiring a director.) Presbytery and/or synod staff should be qualified to give your session guidance on how the proposal should be written and when and where it needs to be submitted.

It is recommended that if a director is hired, he or she be chosen from within the gay community to give your ministry credibility within the gay community. Many qualified seminary graduates who are gay or lesbian are available. Write the job description so that either an ordained or nonordained person may qualify, and be sure to separate the issue of ordination from the issue of ministry in this case. (Some might be apprehensive that once the person is hired, you will push to have him or her ordained. Ordination should be secondary to establishing a ministry.) The decision-making process to create such a ministry should not be rushed, nor should it be overly slow. People, committees and judicatories should not have the feeling of being railroaded, yet the urgent need for such a ministry must be communicated. The decision to develop such a ministry should not be derailed by the presence of a predominately gay church or gay Christian support group in your area. Many gay persons choose not to associate with exclusively gay churches or, even if they do, would respond favorably to an outreach ministry from a church within a mainline denomination.

- **FAITH UNITED PRESBYTERIAN CHURCH**
  430 49th Street
  Oakland, CA 94609

Faith United Presbyterian Church, sensitive to the large number of single mothers on public assistance payments, sponsors a child-care center which permits these mothers to go to school or to work. The center is not operated as a means of encouraging church affiliation but simply to meet the needs of these single mothers. The church is also sponsoring an ongoing Institute of Parenting to assist young parents, single or married, in becoming good parents.

- **THE COMMUNITY FOR CHRISTIAN CELEBRATION**
  1992 Canterbury Place
  Olympia, WA 98502

The Community for Christian Celebration, related to both the UPUSA and the UCC, is an ecumenical, issue-oriented "new life-styles" congregation consisting of small groups interested in the human potential movement and encouraging extended families—married, single, divorced, etc.—to get together around common interests in an informal setting. There is an active singles group which meets monthly. The congregation's weekly celebration (they prefer that word over worship) meets on Sunday evening and its strong focus is on human rights—including such issues as racial and sexual discrimination, world peace, and environmental planning.

- TRI-CLUSTER EDUCATIONAL ARTISTIC
  MINISTRY
  650 Pascack Road
  Paramus, NJ 07652

The Tri-Cluster Educational Artistic Ministry (TEAM), an ecumenical venture sponsored by three churches in northern New Jersey, uses dance, drama, and the fine arts in a concerted attempt to try to reach singles and nontraditionally structured families who have been turned off by the traditional approaches to worship and community. Innovative worship services and programs that "affirm the life-styles of individuals who live in a variety of family patterns" are encouraged.

- PORTALHURST PRESBYTERIAN CHURCH
  321 Taraval Street
  San Francisco, CA 94116.

Portalhurst Presbyterian Church has a unique ministry to the disabled which it calls a "love and care" program. A relatively small congregation of 250 members, this church sponsors programs for the physically disabled and mentally retarded and also helps other members of the congregation be more genuinely accepting of people whoever they are. The programs include regular self-help sessions for the handicapped and bi-monthly dinner meetings and recreational activities for the entire congregation.

- CHURCH OF THE PILGRIMS
  2201 P Street, N.W.
  Washington, DC 20037

The Church of the Pilgrims is primarily a singles congregation with very few nuclear families. It stresses an openness to alternative life-styles including gays. The church had its rebirth in the 1970s when teenagers sought a haven for their nontraditional life-styles and beliefs. Now it is the divorced, singles, and gays who feel alienated from the suburban establishment. The church is innovative in its programs and worship services and believes in integrating its members into its total program—"Singleness and loneliness are the issues for anyone of any age"—as well as providing resources and space for community involvement. The Church of the Pilgrims has sponsored a youth hostel for the past twenty years.

- THE GOOD NEWS COMMUNITY
  2763B, 44th Street, S.W.
  Grand Rapids, MI 49509

The Good News Community, an ecumenical organization sponsored by twenty conservative-oriented churches of the Reformed Church in America, began as a divorce-recovery program; it now reaches out to a variety of people who have become alienated from the conventional church. The community sponsors seminars dealing with such topics as Coping with Divorce, Love in Tension, and Creative Alternatives. The essence of the approach is "how to deal with relationships whether a person is divorced or single or whatever." The pastor, who serves as adviser, believes it is necessary to take certain risks. He is not afraid to frequent singles bars to see what the life there is like. And he believes the GNC should not be closely allied with any church since, whether we like it or not, the image of the church is: "We don't care about singles and we probably will condemn a significant part of your life if you do come here."

Four

Other Models for Ministry

- CHRISTIAN FAMILY MOVEMENT
  P.O. Box 272
  Ames, IA 50010

The Christian Family Movement was organized in the late 1940s by married couples in the Roman Catholic Church. Its membership spread rapidly and was only loosely sponsored by the church. In the late 1960s, following the nationwide trend, it became an ecumenical venture, and the materials developed since that time have been ecumenical in character. In fact, it has been an excellent forum for interfaith couples to share their religious concerns. Membership fell in the late 1960s and early 1970s, but began to rise in the late 1970s, a reflection probably of the conservative trend in the country and a concern for the future of the family. It has never been successful in attracting single parents, possibly because it is perceived as being couple-oriented. At present, recognizing the rapid increase of the divorce rate, it is developing a book, *The Hope and Promise for a New Tomorrow,* which is designed to assist parents who are divorced or separated in coping with the insecurities and shock of single life.

- ## THE NATIONAL ASSOCIATION OF CHRISTIAN SINGLES
  P.O. Box 11394
  Kansas City, MO 64112

The National Association of Christian Singles was established in 1978 as a nonprofit ministry to serve the needs of singles. It coordinates singles programs in over forty states and publishes a "Survival Kit for Singles" which contains helpful hints for single living. The NACS is committed to the position that "all believers are First Class Citizens in the sight of God and that all persons should be treated equally without respect to their marital status."

The quarterly newspaper *Today's Single* is geared to help singles handle their problems. Recent articles include "Counseling the Divorced," "Can You Trust Your Emotions?", "Future Life-styles Predicted," "Accepting Your Singleness," and "Prayers for Formerly Married." The monthly newsletter *SINGLE!* contains information on singles ministers and where they are located, trends in young adult ministries, the times and locations of retreats and conferences for the singles or formerly marrieds, a list of recent articles dealing with singles and occasional bits of spicy information, e.g., a quote from The Reverend Robert Elliott: "Divorce is the only major life trauma for which the church has no ritual, no rite of passage."

- ## THE ALBAN INSTITUTE
  Mount Saint Alban
  Washington, DC 20016

The Alban Institute is a nonprofit corporation begun in 1974 that works with many denominations. Its purpose is to develop healthy congregations through research, consultations, training programs, and publications. Funding comes from private donations, membership, and the sale of its various publications. An important aspect of the institute's activities is the production of resources for local parishes and clergy and for religious organizations that have special needs. The Institute has developed materials for young adult ministry including:

early adult transition ministries (seventeen to twenty-two years old, mostly students and military personnel), single young adult ministries (people in their twenties, alone in urban areas), and thirty-plus ministry (older young adults, often married and parents, who return to the church).

This third area was established with the common expectation that often people return to the church in their thirties after floundering in their twenties. However, a recent study by the Institute's Robert Gribbon seems to indicate that those who do come back—and there is a recent overall decrease in those who do—return in their late twenties. Many of them are hoping to settle down and accept greater responsibilities in their community including participation in the church. The reasons Gribbon gives for this return to the church are similar to Andrew Cherlin's views noted in Chapter One: that there is a movement, typical of the "baby boom" children of the 1950s and of the present conservative trend, back to earlier marriage and having children.

But at the same time this influx is counterbalanced by a growing tendency of the young educated and affluent to leave the church entirely. Consequently a recent Alban Institute publication, "Will They Come Back When They're Thirty Years Old?" advises:

> It will be important for the churches to look at persons around age thirty especially now that the large numbers of the baby-boom generation are reaching that age. We see that many are returning, and the churches will have adults of a new generation to work with. At the same time, there is a very real possibility that many of the best educated in this generation will remain outside of organized church life.

Whether the percentage of dropouts will increase will depend to a large degree on "the responsiveness of churches to the life issues of this group."

Publications of the Alban Institute include *30-Year-Olds and the Church: Ministry With the Baby Boom Generation; Commuter Students: A Challenge for Ministry;* and *The Problem of Faith Development in Young Adults.* Affiliation with the Alban Institute would be extremely useful for congregations that want to be on the cutting edge of demographic changes. Here is what the Alban Institute can offer:

> Our goal is to provide people in congregations with the kind of information and resources they need to support their congregational ministries. Our first priority is to be responsive to congregational issues that you and others bring to us. We don't follow our agenda; we follow yours. When you communicate your concerns to us, we do our best to provide whatever support is needed. Sometimes what's needed is information. Other times what is needed is a professional consultant who can come and work with you. Often as a result of what you tell us, we seek research grants from foundations or denominations so that we can carry out field research on a particular issue . . . Consulting, field research, publications and training are the services we provide to congregations and judicatories.

- THE PAULIST CENTER
  5 Park Street
  Boston, MA 02108

The Paulist Center serves as a kind of "halfway house" for disenchanted Catholics, or a "last chance saloon," as the current director aptly describes it. It carries on a loosely structured series of programs that includes free-wheeling liturgies and much lay participation. It suffers from the same large changeover in membership that all urban churches experience and appeals to many people from a large geographic area who never do join but feel the need for community and support.

The Paulist Center does not have an ongoing singles group that meets on a regular basis; it prefers to integrate singles into the regular programs. But the Director does sponsor lectures—usually four times a year—that are specifically designed for problems and needs experienced by singles. The Center does feature programs of religious education—they are referred to as Recycling Catholic Courses—community needs, women's and Koinonia groups that meet regularly. Many of these groups meet in private homes during the week rather than in the Center itself. The Center's outreach extends to the poor and hungry as well. Every Wednesday evening about 200 people—elderly and street people—eat a hot meal together. The Center also sponsors an annual Greater Boston Walk for Hunger (which netted $175,000 in a recent year) and an annual mass for the "unknowns" who die of cold and hunger on the streets of Boston.

An eminently successful program, which has been imitated in the Boston diocese and throughout the country, is the Divorced Persons Group that meets every Thursday evening. It is both educational and social, with lectures on the problems of divorced persons and encounter groups in which divorced persons share their hurts, each program alternating every other Thursday evening. The North American Conference for Separated and Divorced Catholics originated at the Paulist Center and still has its office there.

The Paulist Center caters to the borderline Catholic who needs acceptance and love but has not found it in the more structured local parish. In the words of one member: "The Center provides a haven for people who are troubled or alienated or marginalized from their own local parish life. Without the Center many people would have no alternative."

- THE UNITED STATES CATHOLIC CONFERENCE
  Department of Education
  1312 Massachusetts Avenue, N.W.
  Washington, DC 20005

The U.S. Catholic Conference also publishes material related to groups with special needs. One such publication is *The Single Experience: A Resource.* This resource has been written by young adults who have a deep commitment to the larger community of singles across the country. It includes such topics as the agony and the ecstasy of the young adult experience; the divorced young adult and a single young adult reflect on the Church. The latter reflection by a single woman includes the challenge:

> With regard to singles, the Church needs to do two things. It
> needs to be the Church for singles. This means being present
> where singles are present, and speaking a language that singles
> can hear. In short it means work. Secondly, the Church needs

to *be the Church.* It must challenge singles to use their energy, talents and idealism in what is often called 'the world.' Think of the possibilities.

Another publication is *Violence in the Family: A National Concern. A Church Concern.* This document provides information about family violence and the resources that are available to those who encounter this problem. Other publications include *Families in the '80s, Planning for Single Young Adult Ministry,* and *Models of Ministry.*

- THE NATIONAL CENTER FOR
  YOUNG ADULT MINISTRY
  Merrimack College
  North Andover, MA 01845

The National Center for Young Adult Ministry was established by the U.S. Catholic Conference Department of Education as a national resource and training center. It publishes a quarterly newsletter, *The Omega Point,* consisting largely of personal interest stories and recommended reading material. It also publishes bibliographies of important resource materials plus other more lengthy monographs. These include *Young Adult Women in Ministry* and *A Sexual Theology.*

- SOLO MINISTRIES
  8740 East 11th Street, Suite Q
  Tulsa, OK 74112

Solo Ministries is the publisher of SOLO, the Christian Magazine for Adults. Solo Ministries is an interdenominational movement, conservative in theological tone. Its bimonthly magazine SOLO contains popular articles filled with practical advice for singles. Topics include "Tips on Beating the High Cost of Giving," "Helps for Building Loving, Lasting Relationships," "Somebody Is Thinking about You," "On Dating Non-Christians and Fighting Compromise in the Real World," "Entertaining the Handicapped," and "Roommates of the Opposite Sex." The latter article advises:

The Word instructs us to avoid the very appearance of evil. And our Christian tradition is that it is not wise for two people of opposite sex, unrelated, to share quarters. Additionally, that is a recent development because in the early church, people lived together without the benefit of bed . . . Paul thought the proper course to improper drives was either discipline or marriage.

SOLO Ministries also sponsors conferences for single adults.

Gay Ministries

There are several national gay groups affiliated with most of the denominations that we have discussed. Although these groups do not usually have official status, they do sometimes receive limited financial support from their denominations and are achieving increasing visibility within their own constituencies. Every one of them is showing a steady growth in membership as gays gain greater acceptance in today's society.

* LUTHERANS CONCERNED
  St. Paul–Reformation Lutheran Church
  100 N. Oxford Avenue
  St. Paul, MN 55104

Lutherans Concerned, a Christian ministry for gay/lesbian understanding, had its beginning in 1974. It estimates that there are more than 350,000 gay Lutherans in the various Lutheran synods. This number does not include their families, who also need support and understanding. Lutherans Concerned identifies itself as

> a national organization of gay and non-gay people who are working within the church for change, in behalf of a Gospel of love, understanding, and reconciliation for all women and men, regardless of their affectional preference.

It publishes a monthly newsletter, *The Concord,* which reports on gay activities sponsored by recent denominations, summarizes books and articles related to gay concerns, and lists resources available for greater knowledge of what gays stand for. One editorial puts it thus: *"The Concord* is a dialogue among us Lutherans who happen to be gay. It is also a means for dialogue between Lutherans who are gay and those who are not."

Another issue told of a certificate "Blessing of a Holy Union" for the "marriage" of gays, a certificate used for the past five years by the Care and Counseling Center in New Orleans. This same issue contains a Liturgy of Celebration. It is "an attempt to collect many of the feelings and fears, hopes and dreams, joys and sorrows that are common to Gay and Lesbian people living in America." Another issue reports on a Family Protection Act before the U.S. Congress that would discriminate against gays. Still another is devoted to a highly critical appraisal of the recently completed study by the Missouri Synod on homosexuality, a study which urges the church to help the homosexual remain chaste.

- UNITED CHURCH COALITION FOR
  LESBIAN/GAY CONCERNS
  P.O. Box 1926
  San Francisco, CA 94101

The UCCL/GC was established in 1972 to provide a ministry of pastoral care, education, and advocacy within the United Church of Christ for gays, lesbians, and bisexuals. The group receives no financial support from the UCC even though it is estimated that there are at least 180,000 gays and lesbians in the UCC plus tens of thousands of parents of gays and lesbians. The UCCL/GC successfully lobbied for the adoption of recommendations by the General Synod in 1977 urging congregations "to work for the decriminalization of private sexual acts between consenting adults," to recognize that "traditional marriage is not the only stable living unit which is entitled to legal protection in regards to social-economic rights and responsibilities," and to "recognize that diversity exists within the UCC about the meaning of ordination, the criteria for effective ministry, and the relevance of marital status, affectional or sexual preference or lifestyle to ordination and performance of ministry."

Mutual networks of support are being formed in UCC Conferences across the country and two National Gatherings for UCCL/GC have been held. The group publishes a quarterly newsletter, *Waves,* which contains up-to-date information about gay-lesbian meetings, workshops, and other activities taking place across the country. UCCL/GC was instrumental in founding MARANATHA at Riverside Church in New York City, an organization for gays and lesbians that has proved to be a highly successful model for other local church organizations.

- PRESBYTERIANS FOR LESBIAN/GAY CONCERNS
  R.D. 1, Box 356
  Hampton, NJ 08827

PL/GC had its beginning in 1974 as an advocacy group for gay and lesbian concerns in the United Presbyterian Church U.S.A. It reported on its activities for the first time at the General Assembly of the UPUSA in 1975, but the General Assembly refused to receive its report for fear that to do so might imply endorsement. During this period PL/GC instituted its monthly newsletter *More Light,* largely as a political forum for gay and lesbian Presbyterian concerns. By 1978 the General Assembly was forced to take action on the issue of homosexuality and, as we have noted, adopted the confusing position that homosexuals should not be excluded from church membership but should not be allowed to be ordained.

PL/GC has become a national organization with a membership of over 400 individuals, both gay and non-gay, and with over 1,500 names on its list for the newsletter. Most of the group's concerns have been focused on the annual Assemblies and in 1979 its annual report was finally received by the General Assembly, giving it a kind of official status within the church. Particularly noteworthy is the fact that the Moderator of the 1981 General Assembly, the Reverend Robert Davidson and his wife, Elder Evelyn Davidson, are parents of a lesbian daughter and active members of PL/GC. PL/GC also encourages congregations to designate themselves as "More Light Churches," indicating their openness to gay/lesbian individuals as full-fledged members and their desire to seek more understanding on matters related to sexual preference.

The newsletter *More Light* contains pertinent information on gay/lesbian activities in the United States. Recent items of interest include stories on the Lazarus Project at the West Hollywood Presbyterian Church (see summary in Chapter Three), a report on PL/GC conferences both past and in the future, and a summary of "A Ministry of Light." This unique ministry was approved recently by the Presbytery of the Redwoods in California and will be a Presbyterian outreach ministry focusing on the needs of gays and lesbians, their families and friends, in the San Francisco Bay Area.

- INTEGRITY, INC.
  4550 Connecticut Avenue, N.W., #605
  Washington, DC 20008

Integrity is the Episcopalian group for gays and lesbians. Established in 1973, it has now almost sixty chapters and over 1,200 members. It carries on a program of parish visitations to educate members of the local parish on the needs and rights of gay persons. Although a resolution in 1979 by the House of Bishops forbade the ordination of homosexuals, more than twenty bishops have indicated that they would not abide by this resolution. In responding to the question: What has Integrity done? one pamphlet answers:

> It has held annual international conventions, bringing together Gay Christian leadership for planning, celebration, and witness, in cities across the land.

> It has represented the Gay Christian Movement to the church—to General Conventions, diocesan conventions and commissions, bishops and councils, and in parishes and missions.

> It has represented the Gay Christian Movement in White House meetings, and provided testimony before many governmental and secular groups in support of civil rights for gay people.

It has established the Integrity Institute for Pastoral Development to provide education and training for the clergy in their ministry with the gay community.

It has published an outstanding periodical of theological and moral discussion, the *Integrity Forum,* since 1975, and has distributed pamphlets and books as well.

It has maintained, with the Universal Fellowship of Metropolitan Community Churches, a Washington office to represent us in legislative affairs.

It has provided speakers for seminaries, clergy conferences, and groups of lay people in the discussion and study of human sexuality.

It has worked with other Gay Christian groups, and gay secular groups in this country and abroad.

It has established chapters in nearly 50 cities and towns in the United States and Canada.

It has, through its officers, maintained correspondence with hundreds of members who have no chapter close by to belong to.

Integrity publishes *Integrity Forum* on a quarterly basis and has plans to publish a regular newsletter eight times a year. One issue of *Integrity Forum* carried lengthy articles by Carter Heyward and Malcolm Boyd, both of them gay Episcopal priests.

- OFFICE OF LESBIAN AND GAY CONCERNS
  Unitarian Universalist Association
  25 Beacon Street
  Boston, MA 02108

Discussion of the extensive program sponsored by this office appears in Chapter Two. This is a rare instance of a gay religious organization officially sponsored by its parent denomination.

- UNITED METHODISTS FOR GAY
  AND LESBIAN CONCERNS
  P.O. Box 25760
  Chicago, IL 60625

UMG/LC serves much the same purpose for the United Methodist Church as the organizations discussed above. It also publishes a monthly newsletter, *AFFIRMATION,* which is similar in content to *The Concord, More Light,* and *Integrity Forum.* A 1982 issue describes a convocation on "Homosexuality and the Ministry" held at Boston University School of Theology.

- EVANGELICALS CONCERNED
  30 East 60th Street, Suite 803
  New York, NY 10022

Evangelicals Concerned is a group of evangelical gays and lesbians and their friends who have banded together to seek gay rights and to make witness to the evangelical Christian communities. Established in 1976, they publish a quarterly *Review* which reviews books of particular interest to the gay evangelical community. They also publish a quarterly newsletter, *Record,* which consists of short news items about what is happening, positively and negatively, to gays across the country. One item told of the shabby treatment members of Evangelicals Concerned received at a recent meeting of the National Association of Evangelicals in San Francisco when EC tried to pass out some of its literature. Evangelicals Concerned also sponsors Bible studies and conferences.

- DIGNITY
  1500 Massachusetts Avenue
  N.W., Suite 11
  Washington, DC 20005

Dignity is a Roman Catholic organization made up of lesbians, gays, and their friends. The membership comprising over 4,000 members is scattered in more than 100 chapters across the country. Dignity publishes its own books (e.g., Brian

McNaught, *A Disturbed Peace,* 1981) and provides bibliographies and other resources for its members. An Augustinian priest based in San Diego initiated the idea of having such a group in 1969 and by 1972 Dignity was established in several other cities. One of Dignity's official publications summarizes the aims of the organization:

> Dignity believes that gay and lesbian Catholics are members of Christ's mystical body, numbered among the people of God. We have an inherent dignity. We believe that lesbians and gays can express their sexuality in a manner consonant with Christ's teaching. We believe all sexuality should be exercised in an ethically responsible and unselfish way.

The following is an excerpt from its statement of purpose:

> As members of DIGNITY we wish to promote the cause of the gay community. To do this, we must accept our responsibility to the Church, to Society, and to the individual gay Catholic.
>
> 1. To the Church—to work for the development of its sexual theology and for the acceptance of gays as full and equal members of the one Christ.
>
> 2. To Society—to work for justice and social acceptance through education and legal reform.
>
> 3. To Individual Gays—to reinforce their self-acceptance and their sense of dignity, and to aid them in becoming a more active member of the Church and society.

- NEW WAYS MINISTRY
  4012 29th Street
  Mt. Rainier, MD 20712

New Ways Ministry is a national group for sexual minorities, their friends, and for the larger Catholic community. It provides workshops, retreats, speakers, and educational materials. It functions with the approval of the School Sisters of Notre Dame and the Society of the Divine Savior. Its distinctive concern is to "respond to the perceived needs of Catholic gay and lesbian people." One of its major services is to provide literature concerning gay people. Its pamphlets include

An Introduction to the Pastoral Care of Homosexual People (a statement of the Catholic Bishops of England and Wales), *Homosexual People in Society* (a statement of the Catholic Council for Church and Society in the Netherlands), *A Time to Speak* (a collection of contemporary statements from U.S. Catholic sources on homosexuality, gay ministry, and social justice), and *Homosexual Catholics: A New Primer for Discussion.* New Ways Ministry takes an active role in promoting the cause of gays and recently sponsored a national symposium on Homosexuality and the Catholic Church held in Washington, D.C.

- UNIVERSAL FELLOWSHIP OF METROPOLITAN COMMUNITY CHURCHES
  5300 Santa Monica Boulevard, #304
  Los Angeles, CA 90029

The Universal Fellowship of Metropolitan Community Churches was established in the late 1960s as a separate denomination that approved of homosexuals and even organized services for marriage between homosexuals. It now has over 170 churches in eight countries, with almost 30,000 members. Its greatest strength is in the larger metropolitan areas. About 15 percent of its members are heterosexual. In 1982 it applied for membership in the National Council of Churches. Although it meets the formal requirements for membership, acceptance is doubtful because, as we have noted, most of the NCC member churches are having a difficult time coming to terms with homosexuality. No decision will be made until at least late 1983.

- AMERICAN BAPTISTS CONCERNED
  108 Santa Clara Avenue
  Oakland, CA 94610

American Baptists Concerned was founded in 1972 as a consciousness-raising endeavor to make known to the members of the American Baptist Convention that gays exist and have special needs. The purpose of American Baptists Concerned is "to unite gay people and their families and friends within the ABCUSA for mutual assistance, education, support and communication." Their newsletter, *Voice of the Turtle,* is published quarterly and includes up-to-date information on the organization's activities as well as book reviews and other information geared to the interests of their readers.

- BRETHREN/MENNONITE COUNCIL ON
GAY CONCERNS
P.O. Box 24060
Washington, DC 20024

BMC was founded in 1976 to help bring about the full accept-ance of gay people by the church. BMC publishes a newsletter *Dialogue* to keep church members informed about gay con-cerns. The June 1982 issue reports on a three-day campus-wide symposium on homosexuality held at Associated Men-nonite Biblical Seminaries in Elkhart, Indiana, in March 1982. BMC has published a pamphlet "What Is an Appropriate Christian Response to Homosexuality?" which states:

> Lesbians and gay men are those who love others of their own sex in spite of the stigma. Accepting their orientation and rebuilding their lives and relationships is a process that may take years because of the many obstacles placed in a homosex-ual person's way. Despite these obstacles, positive and loving models are being developed for relationships between homo-sexual partners. These relationships move far beyond the merely sexual to a rediscovery of natural warmth, camaraderie, and joy among persons of the same sex.

- FRIENDS COMMITTEE FOR LESBIAN AND
GAY CONCERNS
P.O. Box 222
Sumneytown, PA 18084

FCLGC was founded in 1971 when Friends gathered near Philadelphia to form a national organization which resulted in the first general meeting in 1972 in Ithaca, New York. Its purpose is first, to encourage fellowship, friendship, support, and self-affirmation among gay men and lesbians; second, to promote a dialogue within the Society of Friends at all levels with a view toward achieving a deeper mutual understanding and affirmation. The Spring 1982 issue tells of the midwinter gathering held in Washington, D.C., in February 1982 which had as its theme "Closing the Circle—FCLGC and The Society of Friends." FCLGC has enjoyed positive support from those friends Yearly Meetings associated with Friends General Conference, less support from Friends United Meeting (publishers of *Quaker Life*) and none from the Evangelical Friends Alliance.

- *INSIGHT:* A QUARTERLY OF LESBIAN/GAY
  CHRISTIAN OPINION
  P.O. Box 5110
  Grand Central Station
  New York, NY 10163

In 1982 delegates from 15 national lesbian/gay Christian groups met in Washington, D.C. to lay plans for an ecumenical organization. The umbrella group, tentatively called North American Lesbian/Gay Religious Conference, later had its constituting convention in Los Angeles.

The Churches Respond: A Summary

The above list of churches and organizations is, of course, not exhaustive. Other programs and agencies could just as easily have been included if one could take the time to scour the country. New alternative models are emerging monthly. But the selected ones do give an important sampling of what is going on and what might serve as models for other churches to study. What follows is a summary of insights that can be gleaned from the listings in these chapters.

1. No one model can work for every church. Just as First Presbyterian Church in Lincoln, Nebraska, may differ radically in terms of size, character, and membership from First Presbyterian Church in Wooster, Ohio, so, too, will their needs and approaches to these needs differ radically. Similarly, as an individual congregation changes, due to increasing

mobility and uprootedness over the years, what worked in 1980 may not work in 1984. Then, too, what an individual finds important at age thirty may not be the same at thirty-five or forty. Flexibility is a must and no growing and thriving congregation in tune with the times can afford to stand still and rest on past laurels.

2. The wise minister and church board will make a regular survey of the changing demographics of its congregation and community. In my interviews and correspondence I have met too many ministers who have absolutely no idea of the demographic composition of their congregation. Except in general terms, how can ministers be sensitive to the hopes and fears of individual members of their congregation if they lack firsthand information about these individuals? Recently the minister of a moderately sized congregation reported that he was not aware of any single adult members in his congregation. When at someone else's urging he finally sent out a questionnaire, he discovered to his shock that nearly fifty members were single! Accurate information is indispensable for maintaining a successful ministry. The nature and extent of church programs should depend in large part on congregational needs, not pastoral preference.

Important, too, is a genuine sensitivity to liturgical language that is inclusive and is not degrading or inhibiting to certain groups and individuals within the congregation. There may never be a universal language satisfactory to everyone. But it is crucial for ministers and church members to have their consciousnesses raised in this touchy business of proper communication. To a large degree the medium *is* the message.

3. Every category of persons exhibits tremendous variety. I've had divorced persons tell me: "I don't want to be a part of a divorced persons group. I would find that personally stifling. I want to be a part of the total church family." And I have had other divorced persons say: "I sorely need the support of other divorced persons who will understand why I am hurting and whose understanding and sympathy will be so vital in my healing process." This same variety will be found among single adults, single parents, senior citizens,

handicapped persons, gays, and so on. Ministers and church leaders should beware of insisting on only one approach for each special-interest group. Should groups based on age and interest be formed? On the one hand, Robert Gribbon offers his tentative assessment:

> It is not critical for churches to have programs which are addressed to the various critical needs of the age bracket; however, it is important that people hear their life issues being spoken to in some way from the pulpit.

On the other hand, a Presbyterian pastor wrote me:

> In our congregational life we have held numerous intergenerational events with limited success. Our experience seems to be that people want to meet with their own age group.[1]

On the one hand, Harold Ivan Smith, in advocating the importance of a separate ministry to single adults, declares: "The reality is either we minister to them or someone else will. Many single adults have grown impatient." And on the other hand, Nancy Hardesty declares:

> Having participated in church singles groups and having helped start one in my younger days, I personally now prefer to be integrated into the life of the church.[2]

The same kind of debate goes on for single parents, divorced persons, senior citizens, gays, and others. Separate programs or not? Intergenerational or not? I suspect that both approaches are correct, depending on the situation and circumstances. I will have more to say on this issue in the final chapter. What *is* wrong is a rigidity of approach. One minister told me: "I believe totally in the one-family intergenerational approach; we're all in this thing together. I am not in favor of a group for singles any more than I am for left-handers. If anyone tries to break us up and start a singles group, then I resign." That minister *should* resign—from the ministry.

4. Special interest groups—singles, divorced persons, others—are best led by lay people from the interest groups themselves. Ministers are at best facilitators—period. Good leadership is essential, however, for a group to flourish. Whether leaders are young or old, male or female, married

or unmarried is not as crucial as their own leadership qualities and their enthusiasm for what they are doing.

5. Obviously the theological and biblical orientation of a
particular church or agency will strongly influence the character of specialized ministries. A church with conservative leanings, regardless of denominational affiliation, will focus its
programs on Sunday church attendance, Bible study, and
prayer groups. It will attract to its membership individuals
of similar theological persuasion, but will turn off those who
find such groups spiritually stifling. A church with liberal
leanings, regardless of denominational affiliation, will center
on activities of a more secular nature that have as their primary purpose bringing people together for fellowship and
good times. It will play down church affiliation and will attract outsiders who are kindred spirits and have a deep need,
not for hard-core religion, but for an accepting community.

A well-known evangelical minister who specializes in a
ministry to singles has characterized the danger of the liberal
approach to divorced and single persons by saying: "You can
hardly tell the difference between them and Parents Without
Partners" and "For many single adults, it represents a tamer
singles' bar mentality." And he pointed out the potential
danger of the evangelical approach by saying that often there
is "no social emphasis; in fact, some groups heavily monitor
dating or else the leader's attitudes are so accepted that the
dating conforms. Hence the women become 'sisters' in the
Lord."

What seems obvious is that as long as churches and people
differ theologically and biblically, both conservative and liberal groups are needed. Groups need to be alert to a rigid
stereotype that will unnecessarily alienate individuals. And
individuals should find that group that best fits their own
particular needs.

6. Denominational affiliation makes no difference whatso-
ever. This goes for both evangelical and liberal persuasions.
For the younger generation in particular denominational loy-
alty is not important. Almost 50 percent of young adults
change denominational affiliation when choosing a church.[3]
Many of the most successful groups are ecumenical in charac-

ter and have very loose ties, if any, to a national church. This may be due in part to national agencies failing to communicate effectively what they have to offer. Martin Marty notes:

> I am struck that those church bodies which are least self-preoccupied about headquarters seem to be more free to touch the vital faith and practice of their members.[4]

After all, local groups know far more about what they need than do national executives. The ecumenical movement may be dying a slow death as far as the church machinery is concerned, but it is alive and well at the local level. For example, divorced Presbyterians, Methodists, and Catholics have individual needs that far transcend their denominational loyalties. As the evangelical minister quoted above maintains:

> I think it would be safe to presume that the fastest growing churches in America—whatever their persuasion—have nominal denominational ties . . . In one of the major community churches on the West Coast, I found orthodox Jews, Mormons, Catholics, Seventh Day Adventists, Lutherans (of all flavors), Baptists (Southern and otherwise) plus a smattering of others. In the questionnaire I used in working with them, I discovered their lowest common denominator was they felt accepted in their congregation.

7. The critical measure of any successful group is for the individual to feel fully accepted in a caring community. This is far more important than creedal affirmation or denominational affiliation or the particular type of church program. If individuals, whatever their needs, do not feel accepted—if they do not feel like first-class citizens—if they are not loved for who they are rather than for what the church wants them to be—then their churches and groups are failing them. The key phrase, I believe, is genuine acceptance—so-called warts and all. Without this kind of caring acceptance the churches might as well close up shop and admit that the minister is right who said that for so many people the image of the church is "We don't care about you and we probably will condemn a significant part of your life if you do come here."

•Five

Where Do We Go From Here?

There is no question that we are living in a time of vastly shifting moral and social standards, an abrupt transition that Eric Goldman has termed "a watershed as important as the American Revolution or the Civil War in causing change in the United States."[1] Although there will surely be temporary retrenchments, there is nothing really capable of thwarting the social revolution that is taking place. In a summary of his latest book, *New Rules in American Life: Searching for Self-Fulfillment in a World Turned Upside Down,* pollster Daniel Yankelovich states:

> Tomorrow is not going to look like yesterday. In fact, tomorrow—to the extent that research data can yield clues about it—is being shaped by a cultural revolution that is transforming the rules of American life and moving us into wholly uncharted territory, not back to the lifestyles of the past. Irreversible in its effects, this cultural revolution is as fateful to our future as any changes in the economy or politics.[2]

Yankelovich notes the intense social conflict and confusion of the times in which all formerly held moral and social norms are being severely challenged. He estimates that only about 20 percent or so of adult Americans remain unaffected by these mammoth changes—mostly older people in rural areas. But for the rest of us there is no escape from this abrupt transition. Yankelovich maintains that virtually all Americans now believe it is OK to be married and not have children or to be single and have children. Most Americans now say that premarital sex is not morally wrong and that it is quite acceptable for unmarried couples to live together. For most Americans the dual-career marriage has become the norm. Divorce has lost its stigma, with two-thirds of American parents rejecting the notion that parents should remain married primarily for the sake of the children.

And yet, despite all of this turmoil and change, Yankelovich remains hopeful and convinced that "out of the present disorder something vital and healthy is struggling to be born."[3] He believes that a new social ethic is beginning to emerge, an "ethic of commitment," which he describes as "a poignant yearning to elevate the sacred and expressive side of life and diminish the impersonal, instrumental side."[4]

Although some observers predict that Americans will swing back to more traditional life-styles, most would agree with Yankelovich that, although there will be resistance from overly rigid traditionalists, the war they are waging is doomed to failure because the social changes are too pervasive to be short-lived. What is important to remember is that we have become a nation of increasing social, moral, and religious pluralism. No church, no group, no individual has the singular authority to be the arbiter of what is correct and moral in terms of life-styles. Each church, group, and individual will indicate its own preference, but this will not change the preferences of others. A diversity of life-styles will be the name of the game in the future. Not to acknowledge this fact is to try to live with one's head in the sand. We are indeed moving into uncharted territory.

The fact that there are no easy answers is reflected in the splendid report *Marriage Today* by the United Church of Canada to which we have already referred: "We live in a world of uncertainty . . . Clear-cut rights and wrongs are

harder to find than in days past . . . But decide we must lest
. . . we die through indecision."

It is difficult to live with moral ambiguity and intellectual
uncertainty, but we have no choice. In his brilliant article
"Evangelism When Certainty Is an Illusion" Episcopal Bishop
John Shelby Spong makes the case for evangelism for today
in words that we should apply to our own acceptance of a
plurality of life-styles:

> To be honest in our day is to embrace relativity as a virtue and
> to recognize that absolutism is a vice—any kind of absolut-
> ism, whether it be ecclesiastical, papal, biblical or the absolut-
> ism of social tradition . . . We cannot give what we do not
> have. Certainty has never been our possession, but rather, our
> illusion. We offer companionship on a journey and the hope
> that the reality of God will be at the journey's end. But in this
> life the journey will never end . . . The only reward Christ
> offers, I believe, is the Christian life of openness, vulnerabili-
> ty, expansion, risk, wholeness, love.[5]

Like it or not, most churches can no longer make their members believe or act in a certain way. That day is gone forever.
As a 1978 Gallup Poll revealed, 80 percent of Americans
agreed with the statement: "An individual should arrive at
his or her own religious beliefs independent of any churches
or synogogues." Churches, regardless of their theological persuasion, must, in Bishop Spong's words, offer "the only re-
ward Christ offers . . . the Christian life of openness,
vulnerability, expansion, risk, wholeness, love."

How should the church minister to the divorced, the single
parent, the unmarried couple, the gay? I have learned that
this is the wrong question to ask. The person who pointed this
out to me is Brian McNaught, one of the country's best known
"gay Catholics." His recent book *A Disturbed Peace* (New
York: Dignity, Inc., 1981) is an eloquent testimony to understanding the gay person. When I interviewed McNaught and
gave him my usual spiel, wondering how the church should
minister to gays, he interrupted me and said: "You're asking
the wrong question. Don't ask: 'How can the church minister
to gays?' Rather, ask: 'How can gays minister to the church?'
We need to teach you. And only then will you learn how to
respond."

He is exactly right. The church has first to listen to the people in the groups discussed in this book and to learn what they are about—their needs, their hurts, their dreams—before it will ever know how to minister to them effectively. What are these groups trying to tell the church?

The Single Person

The most important teaching in the ministry of singles to the church is that the single state is as honorable as the married state. Mennonite theologian John Yoder writes in Raymond Kay Brown's *Reach Out to Singles*:

> It needs to be taught as normative Christian truth that *singleness is the first normal state of every Christian* . . . there exists no Christian imperative to become married as soon as one can, or to prefer marriage over singleness as a whole or wholesome situation. Singleness is better for those who find their fulfillment in it.[6]

If the church can begin to understand this simple statement, then she will realize that it is inappropriate to plan church services and programs geared primarily toward married couples or the nuclear family. Indeed churches must revise their understanding of what constitutes a family. A recent publication by the Reformed Church in America puts it well:

> We may fear the change in our culture's family patterns. We may wish to recover a previous time. Our reaction could be one of outcry against deterioration in the family. We might as well save our breath. At fifteen percent, we need a new tactic, and the real majority needs to be spared our rantings, despite our inclinations. When we mention family in a church setting, we must make clear to the atypical eighty-five percent that they're as mainstream as almost anyone else.[7]

And the large majority in that mainstream are singles: widowed, divorced, separated, and those who have chosen to remain single. Or to break it down into more precise figures: 54 percent have never married, 18 percent are divorced, 5 percent separated, and 22 percent widowed. Twenty-five million are men; thirty-four million are women.[8]

What are these single persons saying to the church? Above all they want first-class citizenship. They are not an appendage to the church. They are not abnormal nor deviant nor odd. Raymond Kay Brown writes:

> It is my observation that while many singles choose to participate in a congregation, they do so feeling that the church is not aware of their particular needs. They are often expected to participate in established programs, but seldom does anyone seek to discover what is really important to them, or where they are hurting, or what excites them. Many single adults seem to have found a way to participate to a level in their church, but that level seems to be at the surface.[9]

Singles, like married people, are individual human beings. They do have their own specific needs, however, which are sometimes—but not always—met in special programs.

One special need is to overcome the effects of loneliness. William Lyon writes:

> Any counselor will verify that the clients who manifest the greatest anxiety, depression and disinclination to live are those who feel abandoned and alone . . . It is my premise that all but a few single persons want more intimacy and continuity of interpersonal relationships.[10]

Nicholas Christoff notes: "Wherever they are, whatever their life-styles, the greatest problem encountered by single people at every age level and in all walks of life is the depression caused by loneliness."[11] This does not mean that all single people are lonely and all married people are not. But it does mean that solitariness can become a particular problem for the single person. One study has noted that single persons suffer more illnesses than do married persons and suffer more from depression and have shorter life spans.[12] The fact of the matter is that we are social beings. We need to be with other people. Social isolation can be dangerous. As psychiatrist Robert Taylor has noted:

> A very unrecognized factor in whether you stay well or get ill is how connected you are to other people. When we're not in connection with other people, we tend to become depressed and hopeless, which sets the stage for disease, especially the ones we are genetically predisposed to.[13]

If the needs of single persons cannot be met by the churches, then they will turn elsewhere: bars, health clubs, slick magazines (e.g., the new magazine *Intro,* the "single source for single people") with their personal advertisement come-ons, special radio programs (e.g., "Hotline," on WRKO in Boston, which gives singles a chance to vent their frustrations), the Couple Company (a Boston-based organization that features computer dating) and a variety of other media. To those who say the church does not need a ministry geared to singles, one must ask: Why are these other singles groups so popular and continuing to grow by leaps and bounds? These other vehicles for singles would not be booming if singles did not want them. It is as simple as that. Single persons are hungering for companionship and acceptance. They have a deep spiritual thirst to overcome estrangement and loneliness and the sense of abandonment. The churches must listen carefully to what singles are saying and then find the means to serve and nurture them. The church needs to be a caring community which, in Mary Durkin's words: must help those who have been rejected in their attempt at intimacy as well as those who have not been able to take the risk of intimacy."[14]

The Elderly

Closely related to the concerns of singles are the needs of senior citizens. An increasing proportion of the population is now over sixty-five, indeed over seventy-five. And there are 10.5 million widows and two million widowers in the United States, most of them in the upper age brackets. Widowed or not, single or not, senior citizens often suffer from declining physical health and economic well-being. Retirement often brings with it a change of status accompanied by a diminishing self-worth. And the passing years usually bring with them loss of family and friends.

In their ministry to the church senior citizens are asking for a caring community that provides opportunities which, on the one hand, integrate the elderly into the total intergenerational life of church and community and, on the other hand, enable them to enrich themselves through special programs to learn, to socialize, and to serve. As one study has indicated, one's level of religious commitment normally increases as one is forced to come to terms with one's own mortality. Senior citizens should know and hear that in their final years they are as precious in God's eyes as anyone else and have both the responsibility and opportunity to continue to grow spiritually, intellectually, and socially.

The Divorced Person

A recent issue of the conservative magazine *Leadership,* a practical journal for church leaders, contained the personal reflections of five recently divorced evangelical ministers. After sharing a rather enlightened and flexible view of divorce with the editor, a well-known evangelical minister added: "Of course, this is all off the record. Publicly, I wouldn't touch this subject with a ten-foot pole."[15] But divorce is an issue that will not disappear. As *Leadership's* editor points out: "More and more ministers are getting divorced. One recent survey of divorce rates by profession found ministers wtih the third highest rate, behind only medical doctors and policemen."[16] In an article "Clergy Divorce Spills Into the Aisle" in the evangelical magazine *Christianity Today,* Robert J. Stout writes: "Like it or not, we have a tiger by the tail. There may be a strong desire to let go or to ignore it, but it is obvious the problem will not just go away."[17]

Sociologist Dean Hoge notes that for many the church has become a kind of last bastion for the traditional view of the family and marriage.

> We heard over and over the assumption make by interviewees that the church is a natural ally of family life, good child-rearing, respectability and responsible citizenship. Such people feel almost obliged to be active in the church, since the church is a supporting pillar of this life-style. By contrast, people who deviate from straight traditional living...feel strong tension between themselves and the church, and they pull away from it.[18]

Can the church afford to cater primarily to a dwindling number of traditionalists and shun the divorced who, Hoge notes, complain "of little help from the church"? Such a rear-guard action will surely fail. In answer to my question about what churches should be doing for divorced persons, the executive director of the National Association of Christian Singles replied:

> Some of the old-line, fundamentalist churches need to do more to remove the stigma of divorce from their spirit. They really treat the divorced person like an 'untouchable'. And they often refuse to allow the divorced (and sometimes the never married) person from holding official office within the church.

Divorced persons in their ministry to the church are saying that they can no longer be ignored or avoided. The fact that evangelical churches are finally beginning to confront the question indicates how pervasive divorce must be in the mainstream Protestant churches. Divorce is happening with increasing frequency among clergy and lay people whether we like it or not. The question is: What do we do about it? Do we continue to condemn it and instill deep guilt feelings in all divorced persons? This continues to be the attitude of many clergy. As Raymond Kay Brown points out:

> Despite the fact that almost one out of every two marriages in this country will eventually break up, the church and many other social institutions still cling to the belief that nice people don't get divorced. Divorce ...is not for "real people," particularly if they are in the church![19]

Can we continue to be satisfied with sermonizers who point in two directions as they rail against the evils of divorce while seeking to comfort those who have committed this evil? Or do we frankly admit that, in the words of the report on the family of the National Council of Churches, divorce "may become a gift of grace if it moves one closer to the qualities of the gospel with healing"?

This is not to say that marriage should be taken lightly, that it is but a legalized form of gambling that can and should be broken at ease. Marriage is a serious commitment, an intention to love one another "till death do us part." Premarital counseling is important and so is counseling when a marriage begins to break down. Marriage encounter programs can be of great benefit in helping couples work through difficulties which are a part of every interpersonal relationship. Every possible humane step should be taken to save a marriage.

One crucial step in saving marriage would be for the church to support two-career marriages which appear to be the wave of the future. These partnerships usually entail freedom from financial constraints and from old husband-wife role limitations. They also give the couples freedom to grow intellectually and spiritually. The church should be a vigorous advocate of equal pay and rights for women and men and should be careful not to make undue demands of time on the working couple. But, alas, as Wade Rowatt points out: "Unless the working couple takes the lead in calling the churches to this task, the churches are not likely to respond."[20]

Another area in which the church should be more helpful is interfaith marriages. These marriages will continue to increase and there is absolutely no reason why they should have a higher divorce rate if churches are compassionate and understanding. Old barriers and prohibitions against such unions are now fortunately a relic of the past, especially between Catholics and Protestants. Sure, there can be problems, but they are no longer critical. Barbara Schiappa's book *Mixing: Catholic-Protestant Marriages in the 1980s. A Guidebook for Couples and Families* (New York: Paulist Press, 1982) is helpful in identifying areas of potential conflict that can be resolved. Obviously interfaith marriages present a greater dilemma for Jews and other smaller religious groups who are concerned about losing their identity as a people. But even these interfaith marriages are going to increase in this time of religious pluralism. Christian and non-Christian groups have an obligation to play a more positive role if they are going to be agents of marital reconciliation and not disintegration. And exactly the same rationale, of course, applies to interracial marriages.

The divorced person deserves first-class citizenship as much as the single person. The only major difference is that the divorced person has passed through a very difficult transition, the break-up of a marriage, a passage made more difficult because of the negative stamp placed on divorce by society and especially by the church. Thus, the divorced person needs special empathy and consideration.

But at the same time it should be stressed that not all divorced persons are alike. Their needs and problems are varied. Some divorced persons prefer not to be singled out for special attention; they need to take care of their hurts in their own way and in their own good time. Others need a support group to assist them through a difficult transition. What the church should do is not superimpose a "divorced persons program" on the "victims," but rather, learn what their needs are and respond accordingly. What all divorced persons want without exception is first-class acceptance, love, and support.

The Single Parent

Richard Lyman, president of the Rockefeller Foundation, has stated that the growth of American households headed by minority women is now "the most conspicuous and urgent single poverty problem in the country."[21] For this reason the Rockefeller Foundation is making a major effort to train minority women for employment. A federal study in 1980 concluded that "the most important reason for the deterioration in the black-white income ratio between 1970 and 1978 is the faster growth of female-headed families for blacks than for whites."[22] We have already pointed out that forty-five percent of children born in the 1970s will spend part of their youth with one parent, that the single-parent family is now the fastest growing family type in the United States, increasing by over 80 percent in the 1970s. Forty-five percent of all black families are headed by a single parent while 15 percent of white families are one-parent. The growth of single-parent families is due largely to the increasing divorce rate, the decreasing remarriage rate, and the growing number of births to unmarried mothers. Clearly the number of single parents will continue to rise and become an even greater portion of the American adult population. The church has a vital responsibility to this sector.

Single parents in their ministry to the church point out that their needs are the same as single adults, only compounded, because care for smaller children means less time for adult companionship. For single parents the greatest need is often for, in Peter Stein's words: "substitute networks of human relationships that provide the basic satisfactions of intimacy, sharing and continuity."[23] On this point the church should make a two-pronged attack. On the one hand, the church should provide "substitute networks of human relationships" to enable single parents to find adult companionship. This may be in the form of integrating them into the regular ongoing programs of the church and/or providing special programs and workshops that will assist them through difficult and lonely times. On the other hand, the church can provide child care, baby-sitting, summer camps, and other special programs for children which will both give them opportunities for healthy and positive relationships outside the home and also give single parents "time off" to nurture their own personal growth.

Too many children have had their lives warped by "smother" love. And too many single parents, because of an excessive identification with their children, have failed to develop mature adult relationships so essential for their own emotional and intellectual well-being. Both the children and the single parent have unique needs about which the church should be sensitive.

It appears likely that government agencies will provide less and less funds for child care in the future, therefore it is incumbent upon voluntary agencies such as the church to assume responsibility. Increasing concern for child care is crucial for both single-parent families and dual-career families. Here the First Presbyterian Church in Corry, Pennsylvania, provides a model in its "Time Out" program designed for mothers, married or single, church members or not, to leave their small children at the church under careful supervision.

What is imperative is that the church not blame single parents—married or unmarried—for their parenthood as though they only have themselves to blame for their predicament. What blame? What predicament? These adults have made a decision as to their life-style and it is not the business of the church to judge and condemn. The role of the church is to be a healing presence to all of us in our brokenness. Raymond Kay Brown accents the imperative that the church has toward the single parent:

> If the church can help the single parent to care for his or her own personhood, as well as encourage him or her to be involved in a single adult ministry with other understanding friends, a great service can be provided to parent and child . . . The church can also help in practical ways such as being aware of community resources and agencies that can provide special kinds of services for single parents, provide counseling services in economic concerns, and child care for children.[24]

Family Violence

In Chapter One we discussed the impact of violence on the American family. This can include child abuse and violence on the part of one family member against another—including sexual abuse. Much of this violence is caused by undue stress which erupts into physical punishment. In fact, most child abuse is not due to premeditated intent to do harm, but, rather, is the result of the parent's inability to cope with a stressful situation. As one pamphlet on "Families in Stress" puts it:

> Most child abuse and neglect can be prevented: If parents can reach out for the help they need to cope with the stress in their lives. If professionals and agencies that provide services to families can be attentive to families who are having particular difficulties in the demanding task of raising their children. If communities can support preventive programs to help families in stress.

A good agency to consult is the Regional Child Abuse and Neglect Resource Centers located in the different regions of the United States. Then, too, there is Parents Anonymous, a self-help group for parents who want to stop abuse of their children. It is important to remember that most child abusers are known and supposedly trusted by the victim. Indeed as a pamphlet on child abuse published by the United Church of Christ points out: "The abusers may be baby-sitters, teachers, uncles, or aunts, but mainly they are parents."[25]

Churches should be on the lookout for signs of family violence, provide counseling services for both abused and abuser, offer a support group for the abused, sponsor workshops dealing with the causes and solutions of family violence, and be in touch with other agencies that can provide resources in this area. The church should also take the offensive in seeking with other agencies to eliminate those forces in family and society that glorify violence whether it be television, the military, or the gun lobby. A report, "Television and Behavior," by the Department of Health and Human Services concluded that there is a causal relationship between televised violence and aggression. One can only conclude that similar studies of the effects of military participation and gun-related activities would produce similar results. Family violence is not a new phenomenon, but in this time of increasing stress it has become a serious illness which needs immediate and competent treatment.

Ministers and church leaders need to be aware of the symptoms of abuse. The above-quoted UCC pamphlet notes certain signs that children are being abused:

- Appearing to be quite different from others of the same age in emotional or physical makeup
- Being unduly afraid of parents
- Bearing welts, bruises, untreated sores or skin injuries
- Showing evidence of overall poor care
- Being extremely aggressive and destructive, or being extremely passive and withdrawn
- Being wary of physical contact, especially when it is initiated by an older person
- Showing a sudden change in behavior
- Having learning problems even when academic, I.Q., and medical tests show no abnormality
- Being habitually late to or truant from school

- Being always tired and sleeping in classes

Symptoms of abusive parents include:

- Isolation from relatives, friends, community activities
- Seeming to trust no one
- Reluctant to give information about the child's injuries or condition
- Overcriticism of the child
- Unrealistic expectations of the child's behavior
- Believe in the necessity of harsh punishment for children
- Have a low opinion of themselves
- Display immaturity; expect the children to supply the parent with a "parental" type of love
- Seem to lack understanding of the child's needs.[26]

The church has a vital responsibility in the area of child and adult abuse. The United States Catholic Conference in its pamphlet "Violence in the Family: A National Concern, A Church Concern" correctly notes:

> Family violence is a problem which the Church at all levels has a responsibility to address. The imperative to respond is rooted in a concern for human life, human dignity and family life. It is also a matter of social justice. Historically, in its role as sanctuary, the Church has protected those in danger. Whether the harm is from outside the community or from the family within the community, the Church has a responsibility to those whose well-being is threatened.[27]

The Handicapped

While the handicapped have always been with us, they have become in recent years increasingly articulate about their needs. It has been their ministry to goad the church into developing a new understanding of their role within the church as a group with needs as important as those of other marginalized groups. The United Nations designated 1981 the Year of Disabled Persons as a means for increasing understanding of the plight of the handicapped and to work for a society in which disabled persons are given full opportunity to exercise their rights and develop their abilities. This for the church is a practical issue in that it is estimated that one out of four church members will be handicapped at some point in their lives. But it is even more a religious and moral imperative to treat each person as special in God's eyes. The handicapped have a unique ministry to the church. Congregations should survey their members to find out what might be done to make the handicapped feel at home and then to get on with the business of fulfilling these needs. These imperatives include special facilities for the deaf, the blind, those who cannot walk or communicate with ease and so on. But even more, there is need for a community in which the handicapped can feel wanted, accepted, and loved. Every church would do well to heed these words expressed in a resolution by the United Methodist Church:

> To the extent that persons with mental, physical, and/or psychologically handicapping conditions are kept outside of the Church, for whatever reason, the Body of Christ is made that much weaker, and those within the Church, as well as those denied access to it, are denied the means of grace which they could realize in fellowship and growth with one another. Jesus prayed for the unity of his Church. He recognized and appreciated our interdependence and uniqueness. To the extent that some are excluded, all are handicapped.

Portalhurst Presbyterian Church in San Francisco provides an effective model for a ministry to the handicapped. The paramount point to be kept in mind is that handicapped people do not want to be judged by their infirmities. Like everyone else they want to be treated as fully human beings equally precious in the eyes of God.

Unmarried Couples

A poll by Daniel Yankelovich reports that 63 percent of parents of college-age youths agree that "if two people love each other, there's nothing wrong with having sexual relations." Fifteen years earlier 85 percent of all parents had condemned "all premarital sex as morally wrong."[28] The church has always had a difficult time when confronting issues concerned with human sexuality, but it is clear that she is going to have to become more flexible if she is going to have anything positive to say to unmarried couples who are living together. Unmarried couples in their ministry to the church say that they want to be treated as loving partners and not as sexual deviants. This does not mean that the church should baptize everything society does as proper; of course not. But it does mean that the church is going to have to reconsider what are proper norms for sexual behavior outside of marriage. This imperative for a new sexual ethic is underscored by Andrew Greeley:

> Whoever wins the race to put together a viable new sexual ethic which will take into account the perduring wisdom of the ancient tradition and the almost totally original circumstances in which modern Western humans find themselves will receive an enormous prize of human loyalty and gratitude ... I am convinced that any religious effort which does not seriously address the problems and the opportunities for religion in the current ambiguities of human sexuality is going to be a wasted effort.[29]

It is not within the province of this book to give a full-blown theology of human sexuality. However, a few suggestions are in order concerning unmarried couples, the most important of which is for the church to listen to what unmarried couples are saying instead of forthrightly condemning them for doing wrong. Andrew Cherlin notes that

> for most young adults, cohabitation is not a life-long alternative to marriage but rather a stage of intimacy that precedes (or sometimes follows) marriage ... Far from being a threat to the primacy of marriage in American family patterns, cohabitation is becoming more and more like the first stage of marriage.[30]

I am not prepared to agree with the Unitarian minister who told me that a couple who is not living together before marriage has something wrong with them, but I do agree with an Anglo-Catholic priest who told me that couples who live together before marriage probably have a better chance of a happy enduring marriage than those who do not. Indeed, to quote Nicholas Christoff:

> Some of the most vocal advocates of living together are divorced singles who are almost unanimous in their hindsight that living together before marriage could have made all the difference . . . For some couples, young and old, living together is beginning to look like a sensitive alternative to rushing headlong into marriage.[31]

But what about sex for those individuals who do not plan to be married? The church should not develop a casual laissez-faire attitude toward sexuality that makes it the simple expression of a bodily function like going to the bathroom. The church should maintain that sexual intercourse can be fully appreciated only in the context of interpersonal relationships that affirm love, tenderness, commitment and dignity. If we are truly serious in preaching *and* practicing these basic values—and this means no more racism, sexism, and ageism in the church!—then we are on the way to developing an authentic theology embracing sexuality and intimacy. Sex is mysterious and sacred and so intimate that to ignore these values as unimportant is to degrade the beauty and intensity of it all. Daniel Yankelovich points out that his surveys indicate that the vast majority of Americans (96 percent) still uphold the ideal of sharing a monogamous life:

> The stable 96% statistic suggests that when people's experiments with variations on marriage and family slow down, as they will, we can expect the idea of the family to revive, at least in the residual form of the mated couple . . . Couples may or may not marry legally, but they are likely to grow less casual about separating, less self-focused and more serious about the give-and-take needed to deepen the twosome commitment and make it last.[32]

Love, tenderness, commitment, and dignity must remain normative for the Church in all sexual relationships.

Gays

Gays are the modern untouchables. To be sure, gays differ in degree of sexual attachment and involvement as do heterosexuals. Even to talk about gays in a positive way is to invite scorn from many segments of the church. To be gay is to be less than fully human. As one evangelical minister told me: "The attitude of the evangelical ghetto is remarkably evident; unless it is my son or daughter, they're going to hell." The most that can and should be done for gays, according to the traditional view, is to help them to become heterosexual or, failing that, treat them with love and care—the "hate the sin and love the sinner" syndrome once again.

The issue of homosexuality may be, as some people are saying, the most critical problem facing the church since the controversy over slavery. What one national Presbyterian executive told me can be echoed again and again in most of our Protestant churches: "Because of the very sensitive nature of dealing with homosexuality, we do not deal directly in our resources with it. The church is just not ready." The Catholic Church faces the same crisis. As Mary Hunt notes,

> Homosexuality is the most hotly contested pastoral and theological question currently facing the North American Catholic community. It is being debated in closets and chanceries, in seminaries and novitiates, in national gatherings of religious leaders and at the dinner tables in many good Catholic homes.[33]

I believe that just as the official church position affirming slavery was biologically, biblically, and morally wrong, so, too, is the official church position condemning homosexuality as biologically, biblically, and morally wrong.

Biologically? I realize that I am not a trained psychiatrist. I also admit that there is conflicting opinion among competent experts as to the causes of homosexuality. But I accept the views of Alan P. Bell, Martin Weinberg, and Sue Kiefer Hammersmith of the Kinsey Institute at Indiana University who, in their book *Sexual Preference: Its Development in Men and Women,* conclude:

What we seem to have identified ... is a pattern of feelings and reactions within the child that cannot be traced back to a single social or psychological root; indeed, homosexuality may arise from a biological precursor (as do lefthandedness and allergies, for example) that parents cannot control.[34]

If their findings are accepted, homosexuals cannot help being who they are anymore than can left-handers. Some left-handers can be made into right-handers but often, though not always, with negative psychological results. And so it is with homosexuals. Biblically? Sure, there are passages saying that women should keep silent in church, that wives should be subject to their husbands, and other culturally imposed sanctions that no longer make sense. We all "pick and choose" when it comes to the Bible. I am no exception. I pick and choose those passages which affirm love, justice, integrity, and dignity *for all people*. And morally? How can homosexual or heterosexual, left-hander or right-hander, be held responsible for something over which they have no control?

What, then, should be the attitude of the church toward gays? The same as her attitude toward heterosexuals. As Jack Babuscio puts it,

Churches must begin with the premise that no sexual orientation is superior to any other. Such an assumption of equality should extend to the realm of moral responsibility, too—an acknowledgment of the fact that homosexuals are no less responsible for their sexual lives than are heterosexuals. After all, true religion recognizes that sexual maturity and self-realization are essential parts of the gospel of wholeness preached by Judaism and Christianity alike.[35]

The church should no longer consider homosexuality a sin or arrested development. For when churches have taken this view, they have, in the words of Robert Davidson, former moderator of the United Presbyterian Church U.S.A.: "taken a social prejudice and baptized it as a Christian view."[36] To perpetuate the notion that homosexuality is an illness or arrested development is only to encourage promiscuity and hypocrisy among homosexuals. The only gays who can be kept out of the church are those courageous enough to admit their sexual identity; the others the church encourages to be surreptitious out of fear of reprisal. What should the church be saying to homosexuals? Dr. Una Kroll, echoing Brian McNaught's views, responds:

> The Church should not be saying anything to homosexuals. It should be listening to personal testimony, listening to scientific evidence, listening to people who give thanks to God for the way they are made, listening to anthropologists, to poets, to theologians who have holistic approaches to their subjects.[37]

The reason there are so many gay bars and clubs is the same reason why there are so many singles bars and clubs. Human beings need a sense of belonging. They need to be accepted for who they are. If they do not find this acceptance and belonging in the church, they will find it elsewhere, whether they are single divorced, gay, or whatever. Indeed it is a sad indictment of the church that even gay clergy have to establish their own groups—often with the disapproval of their churches—in order to find support and acceptance.

Gays in their ministry to the church want above all their first-class citizenship. This obviously does not mean the acceptance of any kind of sexual behavior as morally permissible. Sexual immorality is immorality whether it is practiced by heterosexual or homosexual, married or unmarried. Sexual immorality constitutes the degradation of another person.

Can gays minister to the church? Can the church respond in a positive way with loving arms? Gays will not go away. They are members of God's family. The church has the problem, not the gays. Let us give Brian McNaught the last word:

> I like being gay. I know there is something very unique and even mysterious about me which separates me from most of the rest of the world ... I like walking at life's edge as a pioneer; as an individual who must learn for himself the meaning of relationship, love of equals, sexuality and morality ... Primarily, though, I like being gay because it is an essential aspect of who I am ... and I like myself.[38]

G. K. Chesterton said that Christianity has never failed; it just has never been tried. That statement continues to ring true. But what is equally true is that the church has failed again and again to adopt her own Christian teachings. She has failed to make the love of God supreme. She has failed to acknowledge that all human beings are children of God and equally precious in God's eyes. She has failed by her acceptance of social prejudices as the normative Christian view. She has failed in her refusal to heed the teaching of Jesus:

> Beloved, let us love one another; for love is of God, and he who loves is born of God and knows God. He who does not love does not know God; for God is love (1 John 4:7–8)

To love one another means to love the married, the divorced, the handicapped, the single, the gay; to accept them with dignity for who they are. If the church cannot do this, then the church fails. For, to paraphrase scripture, if one says "I love God" and then treats the single, the divorced, the gay, the unmarried couple, or anyone else as somehow not fully human, then that person is a liar. For if one cannot love completely each child of God that one can see every day, then one can never love the unseen God. (I John 4:20)

In his book *Embracing the Exile. Healing Journeys of Gay Christians,* John Fortunato writes about the unimportance of sexual preference in a way that can apply as well to every human regardless of status:

> When you are sitting and looking into the face of the Mystery, when you are overcome with awe and gratitude and joy for the overwhelming everythingness of God, and you feel like an empty vessel being filled to overflowing with love, the sexual preference of the person next to you is just nothing. It doesn't matter at all. What matters is that you are both there, looking, worshiping, and being loved by love. Anything else is a distraction.[39]

Tomorrow will not be like yesterday. We are moving into wholly uncharted territory. How will the church respond? The church, as Nicholas Christoff suggests, "has the means and the power to become the healer of the multitude of problems it has been accused of creating."[40] The church can be a support group of alternative life-styles. The church can be an extended family that is all-inclusive in her outreach. The church can be a "halfway house" for those who are oppressed, for those who feel a sense of abandonment. The church can become above all a caring community.

What will destroy the effectiveness of the church is not change in itself, but the church's inability to change in response to new needs. Listen again to these children of God as they minister to the church.

> I am a single adult. I have chosen this way of life. The married state is not to be preferred over the single state. Jesus is a pretty good model for me. So stop trying to get me married off. I am happy the way I am—thank you. Accept me and love me for what I have chosen to be.

> I am divorced. I have had a lot of pain. I am not proud of being divorced; but neither am I filled with the guilt that you, the church, have tried to give me. Don't tell me that divorce is contrary to God's will; don't put this stigma on me. I believe that God understands and loves me far more than you do. And remember—I know a lot of bad marriages that stay together for the sake of convenience or social acceptance or because one or both partners are cowards. I don't believe a God of love approves of such marriages staying together.

> I am handicapped. I didn't ask to be. But I accept my condition. I have no other choice, do I? Can't you understand this? Can't you love me for who I am? Yes, by all means, improve the physical facilities that make you, the church, more accessible to me. But even more important, don't judge me for appearing to be different than you are. God doesn't think I am different. Why should you?

> I am unmarried and I am in love with my girl friend and she is in love with me—and we are sleeping together. We don't think it's wrong. We don't believe in promiscuity. We would not degrade another person. We deplore one-night stands. We have enough trust and faith and love in each other that we want to share our deepest intimacies. Accept us for loving one another very much. That's all we ask.

> I am gay. I did not choose to be gay any more than I chose to be left-handed. I either don't want to or can't be straight anymore than a Jew wants to be a Catholic or a black wants to be a white. I don't like being the modern leper. Would you?

Accept me for who I am: a child of God who needs love and acceptance just as much as you or anyone else.

The role of the church is to be an accepting, loving, caring, forgiving community. The role of the church is to elevate the sacred in each one of us, to revere all living persons and all living things. The role of the church is to become an all-inclusive family in which every member is given full justice and dignity and love. The role of the church is to create that kind of intimate community in which each individual can reveal his or her true feelings to the other without fear of reprisal, but, rather with loving acceptance.

My house shall be called a house of prayer for all peoples. Thus says the Lord God, who gathers the outcasts of Israel, I will gather yet others to him besides those already gathered. (Isaiah 56:7–8)

For just as the body is one and has many members, and all the members of the body, though many, are one body, so it is with Christ . . . If one member is honored, all rejoice together. Now you are the body of Christ and individually members of it. (I Corinthians 12:12, 26–27)

Notes

Chapter One

1. James Hassett, "But That Would Be Wrong," *Psychology Today,* November 1981, pp. 34–50.
2. See the Associated Press-Gallup Youth Survey of 1978.
3. *New York Times,* 18 October 1981.
4. *Boston Globe,* 12 November 1981.
5. Sandra Stencil, *The Changing American Family* (Washington, D.C.: Congressional Quarterly, Inc., 1979), p. 53.
6. *U.S. News and World Report,* 14 December 1981, p. 40.
7. Ibid., p. 40.
8. James M. Henslin, ed., *Marriage and Family in a Changing Society* (New York: The Free Press, 1980), p. 411.
9. *New York Times,* 13 November 1981.
10. Daniel Yankelovich, "New Rules in American Life: Searching For Self-Fulfillment in a World Turned Upside Down," *Psychology Today,* April 1981, p. 58.
11. Andrew Greeley, ed., *The Family in Crisis or Transition* (New York: The Seabury Press, 1979), p. viii.
12. *New York Times,* 1 January 1982.
13. Andrew Cherlin, *Marriage, Divorce, Remarriage* (Cambridge: Harvard University Press, 1981), p. 4.
14. Actually the existence of the ideal unchanging nuclear family in the past is more myth than historical fact. For an elaboration of this point see John Scanzoni, "Family: Crisis or Change?", *The Christian Century,* 12–19 August 1981, pp. 792–799; and Clarissa Atkinson, "The Myth of the American Family," *A.D.,* May 1982.
15. *New York Times,* 18 November 1981.

16. Dean R. Hoge and Kathleen Ferry, *Empirical Research on Interfaith Marriage in America* (Washington, D.C.: United States Catholic Conference, 1981).
17. Andrew Cherlin, op. cit., p. 54.
18. *Boston Globe,* 8 March 1982.
19. Andrew Greeley, op. cit., p. viii.
20. Mary Jo Bane, *Here to Stay. American Families in the Twentieth Century* (New York: Basic Books, 1976), pp. 28, 33.
21. Andrew Cherlin, op. cit., p. 59.
22. *Psychology Today,* April 1981, p. 69.
23. *Boston Globe,* 15 November 1981.
24. Michael S. Jellinek and Lois Slavik, "Divorce: Impact on Children," *The New England Journal of Medicine,* 3 September 1981, p. 557.
25. Ibid., p. 559.
26. *Marital Status and Living Arrangements,* U.S. Census Bureau, March 1980.
27. Andrew Cherlin, op. cit., p. 12.
28. John Fortunato, *Embracing the Exile* (New York: The Seabury Press, 1982), p. 17.
29. Murray A. Strauss, Richard J. Gelles, and Suzanne K. Steinmetz, *Behind Closed Doors. Violence in the American Family* (New York: Doubleday, 1980), pp. 32, 71, 101, 119, 121, 171, 234.
30. *Children and the Family.* Report of the Governor's Advisory Committee, 1981, p. 10.
31. Cherlin, op. cit., p. 33.
32. George Masnick and Mary Jo Bane, *The Nation's Families, 1960–1990* (Cambridge: Joint Center for Urban Studies of MIT and Harvard University, 1980).
33. Cherlin, op. cit., p. 32.
34. *Alternative Lifestyles,* November 1981, p. 523.
35. Ibid., p. 396.
36. Cherlin, op. cit., p. 75.
37. Masnick and Bane, op. cit., p. 10.
38. Letha and John Scanzoni, *Men and Women and Change. A Sociology of Marriage* (New York: McGraw-Hill, 1976), p. 153.
39. Edward Shorter, *The Making of the Modern Family* (New York: Basic Books, 1975), p. 280.
40. Sandra Stencil, op. cit., p. 18.
41. David Reiss and Howard Hoffman, eds., *The American Family: Dying or Developing* (New York: Plenum Papers, 1979), p. 141.

42. Lucille Duberman, *Marriage and Other Alternatives* (New York: Praeger Publishers, 2nd ed., 1977), pp. 54, 69, 22.
43. Sandra Stencil, op. cit., p. 4.
44. *Journal of Current Social Issues,* winter 1977, p. 4.
45. Lucille Duberman, op. cit., p. 130.
46. Ronald Mazur, *The New Intimacy* (Boston: The Beacon Press, 1973), p. 12.
47. Andrew Cherlin, op. cit., p. 69.

Chapter Two

1. Robert T. Gribbon, *Thirty-Year-Olds and the Church. Ministry with the Baby Boom Generation* (Washington, D.C.: The Alban Institute, 1981).
2. *Episcopalian,* November 1981, p. 6.
3. Nicholas V. Christoff, *Saturday Night, Sunday Morning. Singles and the Church* (New York: Harper & Row, 1978), p. 44.
4. Robert S. Weiss, *Going It Alone* (New York: Basic Books, 1979), p. 216.
5. Carl Dudley, *Where Have All Our People Gone?* (New York: Pilgrim Press, 1979), pp. 20–21.
6. Dean Hoge and David Rozen, *Understanding Church Growth and Decline: 1950–1978* (New York: Pilgrim Press, 1979), pp. 68, 105.
7. Martin E. Marty, *Where the Spirit Leads. American Denominations Today* (Atlanta: John Knox Press, 1980), p. 168.

Chapter Four

1. Letter to the author, 22 March 1982.
2. Nancy Hardesty in *The Church's Growing Edge. Single Adults* (New York: United Church Press, 1980), p. 33.
3. Lyle Schaller, ed., *The Parish Paper,* Yokefellow Institute, July 1981.
4. Martin E. Marty, op. cit., p. 232.

Chapter Five

1. *Time,* 30 March 1978.
2. Daniel Yankelovich, *New Rules in American Life. Searching for Self-fulfillment in a World Turned Upside Down* (New York: Random House, 1981). See *Psychology Today,* April 1981, p. 36.

3. Ibid., p. 44.
4. Ibid., p. 85.
5. John Shelby Spong, "Evangelism When Certainty Is an Illusion," *The Christian Century,* 6–13 January 1982, pp. 14–15.
6. John Yoder, in Raymond Kay Brown, *Reach Out to Singles* (Philadelphia: The Westminster Press, 1979), p. 129.
7. RCA *Agenda,* Jan.–Feb. 1982, p. 25.
8. *Solo,* March–April 1982, p. 29.
9. Raymond Kay Brown, op. cit., p. 31.
10. William Lyon, *A Pew for One, Please* (New York: The Seabury Press, 1977), p. 22.
11. Nicholas V. Christoff, *Saturday Night, Sunday Morning* (New York: Harper & Row, 1978), p. 26.
12. *Solo,* March–April 1982, p. 29.
13. *Boston Globe,* 3 February 1982.
14. Mary Durkin, "Intimacy and Marriage: Continuing the Mystery of Christ and the Church" in Andrew Greeley, ed., *The Family in Crisis,* p. 80.
15. *Leadership,* Fall 1981, p. 119.
16. Ibid., p. 119.
17. Robert J. Stout, "Clergy Divorce Spills into the Aisle," *Christianity Today,* 5 February 1982, p. 20.
18. Dean Hoge, *Converts, Dropouts, Returnees. A Study of Religious Change Among Catholics* (New York: The Pilgrim Press, 1981), pp. 170–171.
19. Raymond Kay Brown, op. cit., pp. 34–35.
20. G. Wade Rowatt, *The Two-Career Marriage* (Philadelphia: Westminster Press, 1980), p. 105.
21. *New York Times,* 15 January 1982.
22. Ibid.
23. Lucille Duberman, *Marriage and Other Alternatives* (New York: Praeger Publishers, 2nd Ed., 1977), p. 121.
24. Raymond Kay Brown, op. cit., p. 116.
25. Judith Pavlickko, "A Crack in the Mirror."
26. Ibid.
27. "Violence in the Family: A National Concern, a Church Concern." United States Catholic Conference.
28. Daniel Yankelovich, op. cit., p. 69.
29. Andrew Greeley, ed., *Crisis in the Church,* pp. 228, 261.
30. Andrew Cherlin, op. cit., pp. 14, 17.
31. Nicholas Christoff, op. cit., p. 24.
32. Daniel Yankelovich, op. cit., p. 252.

33. Mary E. Hunt, "Sexuality and the Church's Liberation," *National Catholic Reporter,* 16 April 1982, p. 8.
34. Alan P. Bell, Martin Weinberg, and Sue Kiefer Hammersmith, *Sexual Preference. Its Development in Men and Women* (Bloomington: U. of Indiana, 1981), pp. 191–92.
35. Jack Babuscio, *We Speak for Ourselves* (Philadelphia: Fortress Press, 1976), p. 90.
36. *Nor'Easter,* July 1981, p. 7.
37. *The Concord,* No. 44, Oct. 1981.
38. Brian McNaught, *A Disturbed Peace. Selected Writings of an Irish Catholic Homosexual* (Washington: Dignity, Inc., 1981), pp. 122–123.
39. John Fortunato, *Embracing the Exile. Healing Journeys of Gay Christians* (New York: The Seabury Press, 1982), p. 108.
40. Nicholas Christoff, op. cit., p. 107.

Suggestions For Further Reading

This list includes only recent books. It does not contain numerous journals, pamphlets, and articles mentioned in the body of the manuscript.

General

Gallup, George and Poling, David. *The Search for America's Faith.* Nashville, Abingdon, 1980.

Glock, Charles and Bellah, Robert, eds. *The New Religious Consciousness.* Berkeley: U. of California, 1976.

Greeley, Andrew, ed. *Crisis in the Church.* Chicago: Thomas More Press, 1979.

Gribbon, Robert T. *Thirty-Year-Olds and the Church. Ministry with the Baby Boom Generation.* Washington, D.C.: The Alban Institute, 1981.

Hale, J. Russell. *Who Are the Unchurched? An Exploratory Study.* Washington, D.C.: Glenway, 1977.

Hoge, Dean. *Converts, Dropouts, Returnees. A Study of Religious Change Among Catholics.* New York: Pilgrim Press, 1981.

———— and Rozen, David. *Understanding Church Growth and Decline: 1950–1978.* New York: Pilgrim Press, 1979.

Marty, Martin. *A Nation of Believers.* Chicago: U. of Chicago Press, 1976.

————. *Where the Spirit Leads. American Denominations Today.* Atlanta: John Knox Press, 1980.

McLoughlin, William. *Revivals, Awakenings and Reform. An Essay on Religious and Social Change in America, 1607–1977*. Chicago: U. of Chicago Press, 1978.

Rauff, Edward. *Why People Join the Church*. Washington, D.C.: Glenway, 1979.

Satir, Virginia. *Peoplemaking*. Palo Alto Calif.: Science and Behavior Books, 1972.

Schaller, Lyle. *Activating the Parish Church*. Nashville: Abingdon, 1981.

Wilson, John. *Religion in American Society*. Englewood Cliffs, N.J.: Prentice-Hall, 1978.

Yankelovich, Daniel. *New Rules in American Life. Searching for Self-Fulfillment in a World Turned Upside Down*. New York: Random House, 1981.

Marriage and the Family

Bane, Mary Jo. *Here to Stay. American Families in the Twentieth Century*. New York: Basic Books, 1976.

Cherlin, Andrew. *Marriage, Divorce, Remarriage*. Cambridge: Harvard U. Press, 1981.

Duberman, Lucille. *Marriage and Other Alternatives*. New York: Praeger Publishers, 2nd ed., 1977.

Greeley, Andrew, ed. *The Family in Crisis or Transition*. New York: The Seabury Press, 1979.

Henslin, James, ed. *Marriage and Family in a Changing Society*. New York: The Free Press, 1980.

Johnson, O. R. *Who Needs the Family?* Donners Grove, Ill.: Intervarsity Press, 1979.

Mace, David and Vera. *Men, Women and God. Families Today and Tomorrow*. Atlanta: John Knox Press, 1976.

Masnick, George and Bane, Mary Jo. *The Nation's Families, 1960–1990*. Cambridge: Joint Center for Urban Studies of MIT and Harvard U., 1980.

Mazur, Ronald. *The New Intimacy. Open Marriage and Alternative Lifestyles*. Boston: Beacon Press, 1973.

Otto, Herbert A., ed. *Marriage Family Enrichment*. Nashville: Abingdon, 1976.

Phela, Gladys, ed. *Family Relationships*. Minneapolis: Burgess, 1979.

Reiss, David and Hoffman, Howard, eds. *The American Family. Dying or Developing*. New York: Plenum Papers, 1979.

Scanzoni, Letha and John. *Men and Women and Change. A Sociology of Marriage*. New York: McGraw-Hill, 1976.

Shorter, Edward. *The Making of the Modern Family.* New York: Basic Books, 1975.

Stencil, Sandra. *The Changing American Family.* Washington, D.C.: Congressional Quarterly, 1979.

Sussman, Marvin B., ed. *Non-Traditional Family Forms in the 1970s.* Minneapolis: National Council on Family Relations, 1972.

Wynn, J. C. *Family Therapy in Pastoral Ministry.* New York: Harper & Row, 1982.

Two-Career Marriage

Bryson, Jeff and Rebecca. *Dual-Career Couples.* New York: Human Science Press, 1978.

Bird, Caroline. *The Two Paycheck Marriage.* New York: Longman, 1980.

Dufresne, Edward. *Partnership. Marriage and the Committed Life.* New York: Paulist Press, 1975.

Hall, Francine and Douglas. *The Two-Career Couple.* Reading, Mass.: Addison-Wesley, 1979.

Pepitone-Rockwell, Fran, ed. *Dual-Career Couples.* Beverly Hills: Sage Press, 1980.

Rapopart, Rhona and Robert. *Dual-Career Families.* New York: Penguin Books, 1972.

Rowlett, G. Wade, Jr. *The Two-Career Marriage.* Philadelphia: The Westminster Press, 1980.

Divorce and the Single Parent

Alvarez, A. *Life After Marriage. An Anatomy of Divorce.* New York: Simon and Schuster, 1982.

Arnold, William, ed. *Divorce: Prevention or Survival.* Philadelphia: Westminster Press, 1977.

————. *When Your Parents Divorce.* Philadelphia: Westminster Press, 1980.

Carter, Thelma. *Putting the Pieces Together.* Valley Forge, Pa.: Judson Press, 1977.

Duberman, Lucille. *Reconstituted Family. A Study of Remarried Couples and Their Children.* Chicago: Nelson Hall, 1975.

Krantzler, Mel. *Creative Divorce.* New York: New American Library, 1973.

Murdock, Carol Vejvoda. *Single Parents Are People, Too.* New York: Butterick, 1980.

Peppler, Alice. *Single Again. This Time with Children.* Minneapolis: Augsburg, 1982.

Smoke, Jim. *Growing through Divorce.* Princeton, N.J.: Harvest House, 1976.

Sysar, Myrna and Robert. *The Asundered.* Atlanta: John Knox Press, 1978.

Visher, Emily and John. *Stepfamilies. A Guide to Working with Stepparents and Stepchildren.* New York: Brunner/Mazel, 1979.

Wallerstein, Judith. *Surviving the Break-up: How Parents and Children Cope with Divorce.* New York: Basic Books, 1980.

Weiss, Robert S. *Marital Separation.* New York: Basic Books, 1975.

————. *Going it Alone. The Family Life and Social Situation of the Single Parent.* New York: Basic Books, 1979.

Singles

Brown, Raymond Kay. *Reach Out to Singles.* Philadelphia: Westminster Press, 1979.

Christoff, Nicholas V. *Saturday Night, Sunday Morning. Singles and the Church.* New York: Harper & Row, 1978.

Claussen, Russell. *The Church's Growing Edge. Single Adults.* New York: Pilgrim Press, 1981.

Dow, Robert. *Ministry with Single Adults.* Valley Forge, Pa.: Judson Press, 1977.

Dudley, Carl. *Where Have All Our People Gone?* New York: Pilgrim Press, 1979.

Johnson, Douglas W. *The Challenge of Single Adult Ministry.* Valley Forge, Pa.: Judson Press, 1982.

Lyon, William. *A Pew for One, Please.* New York: The Seabury Press, 1977.

Reed, Bobbie. *Making the Most of Single Life.* St. Louis: Concordia, 1980.

Van Note, Gene. *Ministering to Single Adults.* Kansas City, Mo.: Beacon Hill Press, 1978.

Wood, Britton. *Single Adults Want to Be the Church, Too.* Nashville: Broadman, 1977.

Yates, Martha. *Coping. A Survival Manual for Women Alone.* New York: Prentice-Hall, 1977.

Homosexuality

Babuscio, Jack. *We Speak for Ourselves.* Philadelphia: Fortress Press, 1976.

Bell, Alan P. and Weinberg, Martin. *Homosexualities. A Study of Diversity Among Men and Women.* New York: Simon and Schuster, 1978.

Bell, Alan P., Weinberg, Martin, and Hammersmith, Sue Kiefer. *Sexual Preference. Its Development in Men and Women.* Bloomington: U. of Indiana, 1981.

Boswell, John. *Christianity, Social Tolerance and Homosexuality.* Chicago: U. of Chicago, 1980.

Fisher, Peter. *The Gay Mystique. The Myth and Reality of Male Homosexuality.* New York: Stein and Day, 1978.

Fortunato, John. *Embracing the Exile. Healing Journeys of Gay Christians.* New York: The Seabury Press, 1982.

Jay, Karla and Young, Allen. *The Gay Report. Lesbians and Gay Men Speak Out About Sexual Experience and Life Styles.* New York: Summit Books, 1979.

Masters, William H. and Johnson, Virginia E. *Homosexuality in Perspective.* Boston: Little, Brown, 1979.

McNeil, John, J. *The Church and the Homosexual.* New York: Sheed, Andrews and McMeel, 1976.

McNaught, Brian. *A Disturbed Peace. Selected Writings of an Irish Catholic Homosexual.* Washington, D.C.: Dignity, Inc., 1981.

Pittenger, Norman. *Gay Lifestyles. A Christian Interpretation of Homosexuality and the Homosexual.* Los Angeles: Universal Fellowship Press, 1977.

Twiss, Harold L. *Homosexuality and the Christian Faith.* Valley Forge, Pa.: Judson Press, 1978.

Violence

Adams, Caren. *No More Secrets. Protecting Your Child from Sexual Assault.* San Luis Obisco, Calif.: Impact Publishers, 1981.

Fighting Sexual Harassment. An Advocacy Handbook. Boston: Alyson Publications, 1981.

Justice, Rita and Blair. *The Abusing Family.* New York: Human Science Press, 1976.

Kempe, Ruth S. and C. Henry. *Child Abuse.* Cambridge: Harvard U. Press, 1978.

Monfalcone, Wesley R. *Coping with Abuse in the Family.* Philadelphia: Westminster Press, 1980.

Ray, Maria, ed. *Battered Women. A Psychological Study of Domestic Violence.* New York: Van Nostrand Reinhold, 1977.

Sanford, Linda T. *The Silent Children. A Parent's Guide to the Prevention of Child Sexual Abuse.* New York: Doubleday, 1980.

Strauss, Murray A., Gelles, Richard J., and Steinmetz, Suzanne K. *Behind Closed Doors. Violence in the American Family.* New York: Doubleday, 1980.

Other

Freeman, Carroll B. *The Senior Adult Years. A Christian Psychology of Aging.* Nashville: Broadman Press, 1979.

Gray, Robert M. and Moberg, David O. *The Church and the Older Person.* Grand Rapids, Michigan: William B. Eerdmans, rev. ed., 1977.

Hoge, Dean R. and Ferry, Kathleen. *Empirical Research on Interfaith Marriages in America.* Washington, D.C.: United States Catholic Conference, 1981.

Kerry, Horace L. *How to Minister to Senior Adults in Your Church.* Nashville: Broadman Press, 1980.

McClellan, Robert W. *Claiming a Frontier. Ministry and Older People.* Los Angeles: U. of Southern California Press, 1977.

Perske, Robert. *New Life in the Neighborhood.* Nashville: Abingdon, 1980.

––––––. *Hope for the Families. New Directions for Parents of Persons with Retardation or Other Disabilities.* Nashville: Abingdon, 1981.

Schiappa, Barbara. *Mixing. Catholic-Protestant Marriages in the 1980s. A Guidebook for Couples and Families.* New York: Paulist Press, 1982.

Sessions, Robert. *150 Ideas for Activities with Senior Adults.* Nashville: Broadman Press, 1977.

Vine, Phyllis. *Families in Pain.* New York: Pantheon, 1982.

Zola, Irving K. *Missing Pieces. A Chronicle of Living with a Disability.* Philadelphia: Temple U. Press, 1982.